OKANAGAN COLLEGE LRC
01260710

D1603507

The Canadian Crown

The Canadian Crown

Jacques Monet, S.J.

Clarke, Irwin & Company Limited
Toronto/Vancouver

Canadian Cataloguing in Publication Data

Monet, Jacques, 1930-
The Canadian crown

Includes index.

ISBN 0-7720-1252-0

1. Governors general — Canada. 2. Heads of state — Canada. 3. Canada — Constitutional history. 4. Executive power — Canada. I. Title.*

JL88.M65 354'.71'0312
C79-094254-2

Government Catalogue No. S02-4/1978

ISBN 0-7720-1252-0

Published by Clarke, Irwin & Company Limited in cooperation with Rideau Hall and the Canadian Government Publishing Centre, Supply and Services Canada

Printed in Canada

Contents

Acknowledgements

Even a brief study such as this one could not be completed without much help. Mainly I want to acknowledge my heavy debt to the Right Honourable Jules Léger for his encouragement and constant inspiration. I am grateful, too, for the support of Mr. Esmund Butler, Secretary to the Governor General since 1959, and for that of other members of the Governor General's household, notably Capt. Rychard Brûlé, Dr. R.H. Hubbard, W. Claude Lambert and Mr. Gerald McDuff.

Senator Eugene Forsey, Professor Frank MacKinnon of the University of Calgary and Professor J.R. Mallory of McGill University gave me much of their time and invaluable scholarly advice. I have tried to follow the latter, but I may not always have done so. Any errors, therefore, are mine — as are the opinions. My colleague, Dr. Joseph B. Gavin, S.J., President of Campion College, Regina, spent many hours of what was supposed to be a holiday in Ottawa making suggestions about the style. Mr. Bruce Elliot and Mme Marie Biron helped me with a great deal of the research. The generous, consistent good will of Mr. David Smith of the Public Archives of Canada and Mr. Christopher Stone of the Department of Supply and Services added to the pleasure of working on the manuscript.

Finally I want to acknowledge the support I received from my superiors in the Jesuit order, as well as from Dr. Marcel Hamelin, Dean of Arts at the University of Ottawa, and Dr. Susan Trofimenkoff, Chairman of the Department of History there.

Jacques Monet, S.J.

Department of History
University of Ottawa
Feb. 6, 1979

1
A pageantry rooted in our history

Regularly in Ottawa a great ceremony takes place — a time-honoured scene, a moment of splendour. It is the opening of Parliament.

Enthroned on the dais against the north wall of the Senate chamber, with his wife at his side, the Governor General presides over his court. The prime minister is on his right, the leader of the government in the Senate is on his left, and facing him on their nine scarlet leather chairs are the justices of the Supreme Court clad, as Lord Dufferin (1872-1878) wished, in "red robes and ermine, a dress unheard of in Canada." Filling the Senate are people in colourful formal dress and varied

Lord Dufferin, the first Governor General to travel right across Canada, was appointed in 1872.

10 *The gentleman usher of the Black Rod knocks at the closed doors of the House of Commons, requesting permission to enter.*

uniforms, including Lieutenant Governors, the senators of Canada, privy councillors, members of the diplomatic corps and bishops. Gathered around the throne, wearing their gold, their braid and their decorations are the chief of the defence staff, the senior officers of the armed forces and the commissioner of the Royal Canadian Mounted Police as well as the Governor General's own aides-de-camp and the members of his household. A little below, on His Excellency's right, stand the speaker of the Senate, in black robes and tricorne hat, the gentleman usher of the Black Rod, with his cocked hat and ebony cane, and his deputy, carrying the great gold Mace of the Senate.

The sergeant-at-arms carrying the gold Mace of the House of Commons leads the members of Parliament to the bar of the Senate chamber for the speech from the throne.

On direction from the speaker, Black Rod proceeds to the House of Commons, where the great doors are closed in his face. He knocks three times with the flat end of his cane, into which is fixed a gold sovereign. When the doors are opened, he advances toward the speaker of the House, bowing profoundly three times. He informs the speaker in English and French that His Excellency desires the attendance of the Commons in the Senate. Then he backs out, again bowing three times as he goes.

Following their speaker, their sergeant-at-arms, who bears the Commons' Mace, and the clerks-at-the-table, the Commons members proceed to the south end of the Senate where they take their place behind the bar.

Then, with all parts and groups of the powers that govern us — the Crown in Parliament — physically met together, the Governor General reads the speech from the throne. When he is finished, his secretary, with courteous ceremony, delivers to each of the two speakers a copy of the speech, one bound in red for the Senate, one in green for the Commons. Then the commoners move decorously back to their house, and Their Excellencies and their retinue retire.

Lord Alexander reads the speech from the throne at the opening of Parliament in 1950.

The ceremony is British in origin. Much of the pageantry goes back to England's medieval House of Lords. (The Mace, for example, served the bishops as a battle club and later came to be used by the members of the King's bodyguard.) The closed doors of the Commons recall the fears of the elected members during the British civil war of the 1640s and their claim to freedom of speech and uninterrupted debate. Most of the ceremonial robes are of the mid eighteenth and nineteenth centuries, when lords and commoners in London hammered out the principles of parliamentary reform and responsible government.

Yet as it has developed through Canada's history, the opening of Parliament has become the supreme moment of our country's political life. It exemplifies Canada's status as a united, independent sovereign state.

We know the event well. For over two hundred years — indeed since October 2, 1758, when Governor Charles Lawrence (1753-1760) opened the first Legislature of Nova Scotia — Canadians have been sharing in openings of Parliament. Those of special significance stand out: Colonel John Graves Simcoe, the first Lieutenant Governor of Upper Canada (1792-1796), summoning the first assem-

Below left
Col. John Graves Simcoe was installed as first Lieutenant Governor of Upper Canada in Kingston on July 8, 1792. He chose Niagara as his capital but was overruled by Lord Dorchester, who directed him to locate it at Toronto.

Below right
Col. John Graves Simcoe opens the first Parliament of Upper Canada on September 17, 1792, at Newark (now Niagara-on-the-Lake).

bly to meet at Niagara in 1792 "in the image and transcript" of the mother of parliaments; and the magnificent occasion on January 18, 1849, in Montreal when Lord Elgin (1847-1854) read the speech from the throne in French for the first time. Equally memorable were the historic February 28, 1952, when the Right Honourable Vincent Massey (1952-1959) became the first Canadian to open Canada's national Parliament, and those royal occasions in 1957 and 1977 when Queen Elizabeth celebrated her assumption of the throne of Canada and then her Silver Jubilee by presiding in person over the opening.

The ceremony embodies a multitude of historical events. The two red velure thrones with their armorial bearings and intricate tracery were carved by Canadians, one for the Duke of Devonshire (1916-1921), and the other for Princess Louise, wife of the Marquess of Lorne (1878-1883), and the first member of the royal family to participate in a Canadian Parliament. The paintings on the walls of the Senate chamber represent Canada's sacrifice in the First World War. The landau that bears Their Excellencies to Parliament has carried every one of their predecessors since the days of Lord Grey (1904-1911), and their escort is

Queen Elizabeth reading the speech from the throne during her Jubilee visit in October 1977.

Left
Princess Louise, daughter of Queen Victoria, and Lord Lorne arrive in Halifax in 1878. Lord Lorne was installed in Halifax, as were Lord Grey, the Duke of Devonshire and Lord Bessborough. The drawing was done for the London Illustrated News.

Below
Lord Lorne and Princess Louise.

composed of mounted police officers with their pennants flying our national colours.

A similar ceremony also takes place regularly in each of the provincial capitals. The pageantry is rooted in our history, and in every part of Canada. It shows us that our democratic inheritance descends to us through real people, each with a real role to play in preserving our institutions and expressing our selves. The repeated, measured flow of ritual reminds us that the Canadian Crown and those who represent it — the Queen, the Governor General and the Lieutenant Governors — are symbols of our freedom and our ideals.

Above
Lord Grey leaving the East Block of the Parliament Buildings for the opening of Parliament in 1909. The Governor General had an office in the East Block until 1943. The state carriage was bought by Lord Grey from the Governor General of Australia and was later sold to the Canadian government.

Right
Stephen Worobetz, Lieutenant Governor of Saskatchewan from 1970 to 1976, reads the speech from the throne at the opening of the Legislature in Regina.

2
Head of state and head of government

Unlike the citizens of the United States and the other republics of the New World, but like those in many of the countries from which Canadians have come, we live in a constitutional monarchy. As Queen Elizabeth declared in Quebec City on October 10, 1964, "the role of a constitutional monarchy is to personify the democratic state." Our constitution distinguishes between the head of government and the head of state — between what is divisive and what unites.

The prime minister and the premiers of the provinces are heads of government. They lead political parties and enjoy the confidence

Lord Alexander at Rideau Hall in February 1949, signing the Terms of Union that brought Newfoundland into Canada. Prime Minister Louis St. Laurent is on his right.

of the majority of the people's elected representatives. They are responsible for the selection of their cabinets, and for governing the country or the province. Because they each have the support of a majority in the elected houses, they are masters of policy during a period that the opposition hopes will be as brief as possible. The government rules. It does not reign.

The Crown reigns. The Queen, the Governor General and the Lieutenant Governors sit above the government, at the head of the state. Because they are not elected to speak for the majority, in a democratic country such as Canada they cannot wield political power in practice. Yet they are the source of the government's power. Although the ruling government can dictate how the power of the state is used, that power never actually passes to the government, but remains with the Crown. The signature of the Governor General or the Lieutenant Governor is required to make legal every piece of legislation the government wishes to put into effect. This means that the power of the state is held in a non-partisan office above the conflicts and divisions of the political process. Thus the Crown is a unifying force. In the words of the Right Honourable

The Fathers of Confederation met in London in 1866 to frame the British North America Act. Painting by J.D. Kelly.

Vincent Massey, "it represents equally all the elements which make up the state." In addition, because they are not limited by party loyalties and the necessary compromises of politics, the representatives of the Crown help us to separate our quarrels from our common beliefs.

The Fathers of Confederation were quite emphatic about the need for such a separation between the offices of head of state and head of government. Speaking during the debate on Confederation in 1865, the former Prime Minister of the Province of Canada, Sir George-Etienne Cartier, declared, "our pur-

BY THE QUEEN.

A PROCLAMATION

For Uniting the Provinces of Canada, Nova Scotia, and New Brunswick into One Dominion under the Name of CANADA.

VICTORIA R.

WHEREAS by an Act of Parliament passed on the Twenty-ninth Day of March One thousand eight hundred and sixty-seven, in the Thirtieth Year of Our Reign, intituled "An Act for the Union of Canada, Nova Scotia, and New Brunswick, and the "Government thereof, and for Purposes connected therewith," after divers Recitals, it is enacted, that "it shall be lawful for the Queen, by and with the Advice of Her Majesty's most Honorable "Privy Council, to declare by Proclamation that on and after a Day therein appointed, not being "more than Six Months after the passing of this Act, the Provinces of Canada, Nova Scotia, and "New Brunswick shall form and be One Dominion under the Name of Canada, and on and after "that Day those Three Provinces shall form and be One Dominion under that Name accordingly:" And it is thereby further enacted, that "such Persons shall be first summoned to the Senate as "the Queen, by Warrant under Her Majesty's Royal Sign Manual, thinks fit to approve, and "their Names shall be inserted in the Queen's Proclamation of Union:" We therefore, by and with the Advice of Our Privy Council, have thought fit to issue this Our Royal Proclamation, and We do Ordain, Declare, and Command, that on and after the First Day of July One thousand eight hundred and sixty-seven the Provinces of Canada, Nova Scotia, and New Brunswick shall form and be One Dominion under the Name of Canada. And We do further Ordain and Declare, that the Persons whose Names are herein inserted and set forth are the Persons of whom We have, by Warrant under Our Royal Sign Manual, thought fit to approve as the Persons who shall be first summoned to the Senate of Canada.

FOR THE PROVINCE OF ONTARIO.	FOR THE PROVINCE OF QUEBEC.	FOR THE PROVINCE OF NOVA SCOTIA.	FOR THE PROVINCE OF NEW BRUNSWICK.
JOHN HAMILTON,	JAMES LESLIE,	EDWARD KENNY,	AMOS EDWIN BOTSFORD,
RODERICK MATHESON,	ASA BELKNAP FOSTER,	JONATHAN M'CULLY,	EDWARD BARRON CHANDLER,
JOHN ROSS,	JOSEPH NOËL BOSSÉ,	THOMAS D. ARCHIBALD,	JOHN ROBERTSON,
SAMUEL MILLS,	LOUIS A. OLIVIER,	ROBERT B. DICKEY,	ROBERT LEONARD HAZEN,
BENJAMIN SEYMOUR,	JACQUE OLIVIER BUREAU,	JOHN H. ANDERSON,	WILLIAM HUNTER ODELL,
WALTER HAMILTON DICKSON,	CHARLES MALHIOT,	JOHN HOLMES,	DAVID WARK,
JAMES SHAW,	LOUIS RENAUD,	JOHN W. RITCHIE,	WILLIAM HENRY STEEVES,
ADAM JOHNSTON FERGUSON BLAIR,	LUC LETELLIER DE ST. JUST,	BENJAMIN WIER,	WILLIAM TODD,
ALEXANDER CAMPBELL,	ULRIC JOSEPH TESSIER,	JOHN LOCKE,	JOHN FERGUSON,
DAVID CHRISTIE,	JOHN HAMILTON,	CALEB R. BILL,	ROBERT DUNCAN WILMOT,
JAMES COX AIKINS,	CHARLES CORMIER,	JOHN BOURINOT,	ABNER REID M'CLELAN,
DAVID REESOR,	ANTOINE JUCHEREAU DUCHESNAY,	WILLIAM MILLER.	PETER MITCHELL.
ELIJAH LEONARD,	DAVID EDWARD PRICE,		
WILLIAM MACMASTER,	ELZEAR H. J. DUCHESNAY,		
ASA ALLWORTH BURNHAM,	LEANDRE DUMOUCHEL,		
JOHN SIMPSON,	LOUIS LACOSTE,		
JAMES SKEAD,	JOSEPH F. ARMAND,		
DAVID LEWIS MACPHERSON,	CHARLES WILSON,		
GEORGE CRAWFORD,	WILLIAM HENRY CHAFFERS,		
DONALD MACDONALD,	JEAN BAPTISTE GUÉVREMONT,		
OLIVER BLAKE,	JAMES FERRIER,		
BILLA FLINT,	Sir NARCISSE FORTUNAT BELLEAU, Knight,		
WALTER M'CREA,	THOMAS RYAN,		
GEORGE WILLIAM ALLAN.	JOHN SEWELL SANBORN.		

Given at Our Court at Windsor Castle, this Twenty-second Day of May, in the Year of our Lord One thousand eight hundred and sixty-seven, and in the Thirtieth Year of Our Reign.

God save the Queen.

Queen Victoria's proclamation of Confederation, 1867.

pose in forming a federation is to perpetuate the monarchical element. In our federation the monarchical principle will form the leading feature...." Later in the same debate, Sir John A. Macdonald elaborated:

By adhering to the monarchical principle, we avoid one defect inherent in the Constitution of the United States. By the election of the President by a majority and for a short period, he never is the Sovereign and the Chief of the nation. He is never looked up to by the whole people as the head and front of the nation. He is at best the successful leader of a party.... This defect is all the greater because of the practice of re-election. During his first term of office, he is employed in taking steps to secure his own re-election, and for his party a continuance of power. We avoid this by adhering to the monarchical principle — the Sovereign whom you respect and love. I believe that it is of the utmost importance to have that principle recognized, so that we shall have a Sovereign who is placed above the region of party — to whom all parties look up — who is not elevated by the action of one party nor depressed by the action of another, who is the common head and sovereign of all.

And it is precisely the same point which Cardinal Roy of Quebec chose to underline a century later, in his eulogy for Lieutenant Governor Paul Comtois of Quebec (1961-1966):

In his person the authority of the state was at once dignified and familiar; concerned to radiate joy as much

Viscount Monck played an important part in the events that led to Confederation. He is seen here (third from left) on the ramparts of Quebec in August 1862 with Arthur Hamilton Gordon, Lieutenant Governor of New Brunswick (second from left), and the Earl of Mulgrave, Lieutenant Governor of Nova Scotia (second from right).

as to inspire respect. It is important that above the necessary discussions and inevitable clashes of a democratic society, the authority of the state, which is a gift from God, appear in all its richness, and that it be not only strong and noble but also generous and kind.

The Fathers of Confederation wanted a head of state who was "respectable" in the political sense — someone who was entirely dissociated from any involvement in partisan controversy. The highest office in the country would be beyond contest and would bind the new nation with ties of gratitude and affection.

When the Crown ruled

The distinction between a representative head of state and an active, political head of government was a novelty for the Fathers of Confederation. It was at the beginning of their own generation that it had first been drawn. All of them were born in the reign of monarchs who wielded at least some power, and all of them had begun their own careers under governors who actively exercised political control. In fact, from the beginning of Canada's history up to that time, Canada's monarchs and governors had ruled as well as reigned.

Above
Bois-de-Coulonge, official residence of the Lieutenant Governors of Quebec from 1867 to 1966. Formerly called Spencerwood, the historic mansion was built in 1862 and was destroyed by fire in 1966.

Below
Paul Comtois, Lieutenant Governor of Quebec from 1961 to 1966, died tragically in February 1966 in the fire which destroyed his official residence.

The traditions were ancient. King Henry VII (1485-1509) of England followed carefully the lengthy process by which agreement was reached on the terms of the Letters Patent which he signed on March 5, 1496, for John Cabot, who "discovered" Newfoundland and then asserted his King's rights over its riches. Likewise in 1534 François I (1515-1547) of France personally ordered Jacques Cartier to leave for the lands which, on the point of Gaspé, on July 24, were to be claimed for his Crown. Much later, Charles II (1660-1685), on May 2, 1670, granted a charter to the Hudson's Bay Company — a company that was to rule over most of Canada's territory for two centuries.

Henri IV (1589-1610) of France gave precise instructions to Champlain before the founder of Quebec set sail for Acadia in 1604 and then for New France in 1608. Yet it was Louis XIV (1643-1715), the Sun King, who more than any other monarch except perhaps Queen Victoria (1837-1901) two centuries later, put his imprint on Canadian society. In 1663 he made New France a royal province to be governed directly under his control. He saw to the shipment of teachers and craftsmen, stimulated industry and land settlement, and

Henry VII honoured John Cabot for his discoveries in North America. The explorer had claimed the lands for his King in 1497. Painting by J.D. Kelly.

personally encouraged and rewarded the missionaries and explorers who dotted his royal fleur-de-lis across the map of North America from Hudson Bay to New Orleans and from Acadia westwards "as far away and forward as they can possibly go to make known the name of His Majesty." It was through his efforts, and those of his descendant, Louis XV (1715-1760), that French Canadian society took root. Church and state were secured. The *habitants* were established on the land along the St. Lawrence with their family traditions and their own laws and customs. New "*canadien*" patterns of art and architecture emerged, as well as a language with a different accent, and novel patterns of social and religious life. Many of these traits, as Dr. W.J. Eccles has noted in his study of the age of Louis XIV,

> were to endure until the conquest in 1760. Even then some of these values and attitudes towards life were not completely destroyed, they were too deep-rooted.... Something of their essence always persisted to perplex, at times, Canadians of other than French descent.

George III (1760-1820) paid scrupulous attention to the passage of the Quebec Act of 1774, in which were recognized and given a firm constitutional foundation the civil laws, as well as the religious rights and social

Below
Sir Guy Carleton's proclamation of the Quebec Act, 1774.

Above
Acting on a commission from François I, Jacques Cartier landed on the shores of the Gaspé Peninsula in July 1534 and planted a cross claiming the land for his sovereign. Painting by J.D. Kelly.

By His EXCELLENCY
GUY CARLETON,
Captain General and Governor in Chief in and over the Province of Quebec, *and the Territories depending thereon in* America, *Vice Admiral of the ſame; and Major General of His Majeſty's Forces Commanding the Northern Diſtrict, &c. &c.*

A PROCLAMATION.

HIS Majeſty's Secretary of State having tranſmitted to me two Acts paſſed in the laſt Seſſion of Parliament, Intituled,
"An Act for making more effectual Proviſion for the Government of the Province of *Quebec* in *North America,*" And
"An Act to eſtabliſh a Fund towards further defraying the Charges of the Adminiſtration of Juſtice, and Support of the Civil Government within the Province of *Quebec*, in *America*;"
I have thought fit to publiſh the ſame, that all Officers Civil and Military, and others, whom they concern, may take Notice thereof, and Govern themſelves Accordingly.

Given under my Hand and Seal at Arms, at the Caſtle of Saint Lewis, *in the City of* Quebec, *the Eighth Day of* December, *One thouſand ſeven hundred and ſeventy-four, in the Fifteenth Year of the Reign of our Sovereign Lord* George *the Third, by the Grace of God, of* Great Britain, France, *and* Ireland, *King, Defender of the Faith, and ſo forth.*

GUY CARLETON.

By his Excellency's Command,
GEO. ALLSOPP, D. Secy.
GOD ſave the KING.

institutions, of his "new" French-Canadian subjects. He was personally involved in the land grants to the Loyalists in what was to become Upper Canada (later Ontario), in the foundation of the Province of New Brunswick in 1784, and in the great land grant to the Six Nations on the Grand River.

Toward the end of his life, and during the reigns of his two sons George IV (1820-1830) and William IV (1830-1837), the Crown's political power passed to the British prime minister. As that happened, the distinction between the power of the head of government and the reign of the head of state grew more and more obvious.

When Governors ruled

Since the days of Champlain (1627-1635), Canada's kings and queens had exercised their power from a distance and by proxy. They sent governors to carry out their instructions or to rule in their name. Gradually the office of Governor General began to develop a character of its own. The title — Governor, Governor-in-Chief, Lieutenant Governor, Governor General — and the responsibilities varied, as did the extent of the territories over which they were exercised. But without a break since the beginning of European settlement in Canada, the Governor General has stood at the head of

Below left
The Quebec Council of 1775. The Quebec Act of 1774 set up an appointed council to govern Quebec. It met for the first time in the ancient residence of the Governor, the Chateau St. Louis, in August 1775.

Below right
The Duke of Connaught (centre) in 1911 at the Mohawk Chapel outside Brantford on the land granted to the Mohawk nation in 1784 by Governor Haldimand.

the state as the senior resident representative of the Crown. In fact, the office of Governor General is the only institution in Canada today which serves as an uninterrupted link with the beginnings of Canada's recorded history.

Champlain began it all. With his enthusiasm and his many talents — he was at different times and sometimes all at once a sailor, soldier, botanist, artist, architect, governor and expert in agriculture — he set out to create a new world. He hoped from Quebec to establish a great kingdom that would encompass the resources and commerce of the vast hinterlands that extended westwards, as he wrote, "as far as they can go." He set the pattern for

Samuel de Champlain, born in France, came to Canada in 1603. After spending several years in Acadia, he founded Quebec in 1608. Before his death in 1635 he explored much of the St. Lawrence and what is now south-central Ontario and upper New York State.

what would become some of the most distinctive traits of Canada's character: those of a courageous people, small in number, politically rooted in the old world, collected in isolated communities in a large country, preserving their identity next to neighbours vastly greater in number.

It was Champlain who laid the groundwork for the Royal Government that Louis XIV officially proclaimed in 1663 — the first of our many "constitutional" steps toward full Canadian sovereignty. The Governor General, appointed by the King to represent his person, was the highest dignitary in the land. His authority extended to all French possessions in North America, and it was he who appointed the commanders of all the forts and trading posts in the territories of the West. Among his other duties, he was especially commissioned to direct all military administration and command the troops. He also held the ultimate responsibility for all relations with the native peoples. From the King he had at his disposal the sum of ten thousand *livres*, an amount that section 105 of the British North America Act sets as the salary for the Governor General of Canada.

Louis de Frontenac (1672-1682, 1689-

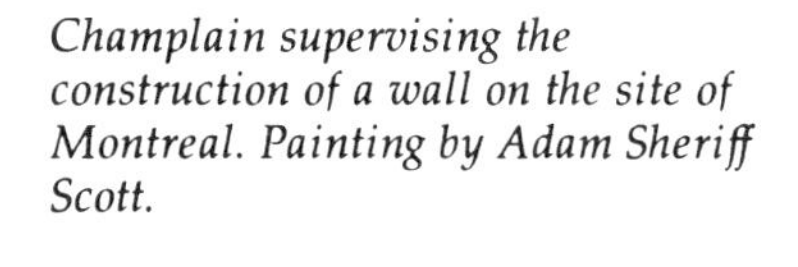

Champlain supervising the construction of a wall on the site of Montreal. Painting by Adam Sheriff Scott.

1698), probably the most powerful of the Governors during the French regime, and certainly the most influential, fulfilled Champlain's dream. He settled the "long continuous village" along the St. Lawrence and sent explorers and traders out to claim the lands of Louisiana and the prairies. Before his death he had opened up a new empire, overseeing the export of up to 500,000 pounds of beaver pelt per year. His successor, Hector de Callière (1698-1703), negotiated the great Treaty of Montreal in 1701, where some 1,300 Indians from over thirty tribes located as far apart as the Atlantic coast and the Mississippi assembled to recognize the Governor General as the arbiter and protector of the rights of all the native peoples.

Pierre de Vaudreuil (1755-1760), the first Governor General to have been born in Canada, was, ironically, the last of the French regime. It was he who surrendered to Jeffrey Amherst, the first of the British governors (1760-1763). He handed over to his successor his responsibility for all civil and military matters, as well as Indian affairs. In addition he bequeathed to him many of the values of New France — those of an organized society, of balanced institutions, of decency, honour and the

Below left
Pierre de Rigaud de Vaudreuil de Cavagnial, the first Canadian-born Governor General, was appointed in 1755. His main concern during his term was the defence of Canada.

Below centre
Sir Jeffery Amherst, the first British Governor General, to whom Vaudreuil surrendered in 1760. His command extended from Virginia to Hudson Bay.

Above
Sir Guy Carleton, Lord Dorchester, Governor of Canada for two terms. He recommended the Quebec Act of 1774, repulsed the American invasion, and later helped with the settlement of the Loyalists.

Vaudreuil surrendered to Amherst at Montreal in 1760. This painting by Adam Sheriff Scott shows Amherst receiving the keys of the city from Vaudreuil at Place d'Armes.

Lord Elgin began the practice of responsible government in Canada in 1848. Here he is pictured in the Legislative Council at Quebec giving royal assent. During this ceremony the title of each law is read aloud and the Governor General nods his head in assent.

acceptance of a duty that calls for service beyond the advantages of self.

General James Murray (1764-1768) and Sir Guy Carleton, later Lord Dorchester (1768-1778, 1786-1796), accepted the bequest. The Quebec Act of 1774 confirmed the nationality and institutions of French Canada. Then, by safeguarding the settlement of the Loyalists and other immigrants, Lord Dorchester also secured the foundation of a British society in Canada. After the Constitutional Act of 1791 established assemblies in Upper and Lower Canada, he and his successors ruled in these parliaments until 1848. In that year Lord Elgin gave new meaning to the power of his office. Responding to the pressures of Canadian politics, he decided to appoint as prime minister a political leader who had the confidence of the elected assembly. In all local matters the Governor would follow the "advice" of this leader. A few weeks earlier Sir John Harvey (1846-1852), Lieutenant Governor of Nova Scotia, had done likewise.

From that time, the Governor General and the Lieutenant Governors, like the King, would reign more than they would rule. However, in Canada as in Britain, these changes in the Crown's role were often the result of much

Below left
Sir John Harvey was, at various times, Governor of each of the Atlantic provinces. In 1848, in Nova Scotia, he became the first Governor to introduce fully responsible government.

Below right
The Last Great Council of the West, 1881. Chief Crowfoot of the Blackfoot Indians meets with Lord Lorne at Blackfoot Crossing near Calgary. The special relationship between the native people and the Governor General has continued to the present day.

friction and violence. Champlain and the Marquis de Denonville (1685-1689) provoked wars with the native peoples. Lieutenant Governor Charles Lawrence gave the orders for the deportation of the Acadians in 1755. Sir John Colborne (1838-1839) earned the nickname "the old firebrand" because of the forceful manner in which he repressed the rebellion of 1838 in Lower Canada, much as Sir Francis Bond Head's (1836-1838) arrogance had aggravated the political climate that led to the rebellion of 1837 in Upper Canada. Lord Elgin was almost stoned to death by an angry mob that had burned down the Parliament Buildings in Montreal to mark their disapproval of his commitment to follow the advice of a prime minister. Yet by 1850 Canadians and their governors were educated in the difference between the head of government and the head of state. The Governor General could reign independent of social and political divisions as a sign of unity and a bond of integrity.

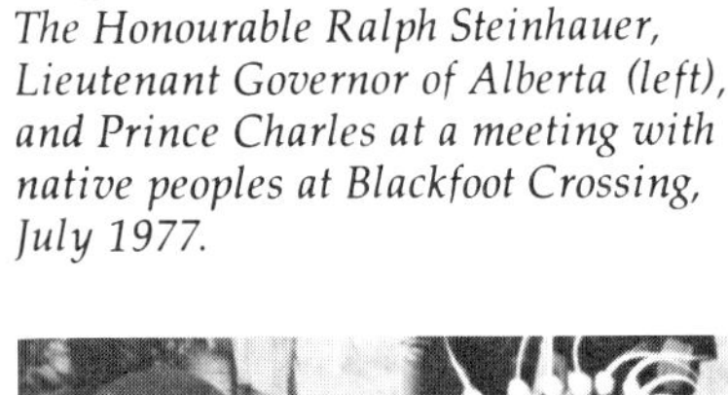
Below
The Honourable Ralph Steinhauer, Lieutenant Governor of Alberta (left), and Prince Charles at a meeting with native peoples at Blackfoot Crossing, July 1977.

Right
Big Eagle. General Vanier in Calgary, 1965.

PROCLAMATION.

BY His Excellency SIR FRANCIS BOND HEAD, Baronet, Lieutenant Governor of Upper Canada, &c. &c.

To the Queen's Faithful Subjects in Upper Canada.

In a time of profound peace, while every one was quietly following his occupations, feeling secure under the protection of our Laws, a band of Rebels, instigated by a few malignant and disloyal men, has had the wickedness and audacity to assemble with Arms, and to attack and Murder the Queen's Subjects on the Highway—to Burn and Destroy their Property—to Rob the Public Mails—and to threaten to Plunder the Banks—and to Fire the City of Toronto.

Brave and Loyal People of Upper Canada, we have been long suffering from the acts and endeavours of concealed Traitors, but this is the first time that Rebellion has dared to shew itself openly in the land, in the absence of invasion by any Foreign Enemy.

Let every man do his duty now, and it will be the last time that we or our children shall see our lives or properties endangered, or the Authority of our Gracious Queen insulted by such treacherous and ungrateful men. MILITIA-MEN OF UPPER CANADA, no Country has ever shewn a finer example of Loyalty and Spirit than YOU have given upon this sudden call of Duty. Young and old of all ranks, are flocking to the Standard of their Country. What has taken place will enable our Queen to know Her Friends from Her Enemies—a public enemy is never so dangerous as a concealed Traitor—and now my friends let us complete well what is begun—let us not return to our rest till Treason and Traitors are revealed to the light of day, and rendered harmless throughout the land.

Be vigilant, patient and active—leave punishment to the Laws—our first object is, to arrest and secure all those who have been guilty of Rebellion, Murder and Robbery.—And to aid us in this, a Reward is hereby offered of

One Thousand Pounds,

to any one who will apprehend, and deliver up to Justice, WILLIAM LYON MACKENZIE; and FIVE HUNDRED POUNDS to any one who will apprehend, and deliver up to Justice, DAVID GIBSON—or SAMUEL LOUNT—or JESSE LLOYD—or SILAS FLETCHER—and the same reward and a free pardon will be given to any of their accomplices who will render this public service, except he or they shall have committed, in his own person, the crime of Murder or Arson.

And all, but the Leaders above-named, who have been seduced to join in this unnatural Rebellion, are hereby called to return to their duty to their Sovereign—to obey the Laws—and to live henceforward as good and faithful Subjects—and they will find the Government of their Queen as indulgent as it is just.

GOD SAVE THE QUEEN.

Thursday, 3 o'clock, P. M.
7th Dec.

☞ **The Party of Rebels, under their Chief Leaders, is wholly dispersed, and flying before the Loyal Militia. The only thing that remains to be done, is to find them, and arrest them.**

R. STANTON, Printer to the QUEEN'S Most Excellent Majesty.

Proclamation by Sir Francis Bond Head, Lieutenant Governor of Upper Canada. During the rebellions of 1837 and 1838, the Governors in Upper and Lower Canada took measures to restore order. This proclamation called for the arrest of William Lyon Mackenzie.

3
A Canadian choice

The evolution in the role of the Crown's representatives set the constitutional stage for Confederation. As we have seen, the Fathers gathered at Charlottetown and then at Quebec deliberately decided to retain what they called "the British system," which separated the exercise of power by politicians from the reign of the Crown. The Honourable Eugene Forsey emphasized this in a speech to the Senate on March 29, 1972:

> The first thing I want to say about the existing monarchy in this country is the fact that it exists is once again our own decision. It is not something which was adopted in a fit of absent-mindedness by the Fathers of Confederation or because they were colonial minded

The Fathers of Confederation gathered at Charlottetown on September 1, 1864.

or because they were stupid or because they were ignorant. It was deliberately adopted by the Fathers of Confederation, unanimously and with their eyes wide open.

Here is what Sir John A. Macdonald had to say on the subject ... :

"If therefore at the Conference, we had arrived at the conclusion, that it was for the interest —"

And observe the word "interest", not "sentiment", not "tradition" — "interest"

"— of these provinces that a severance should take place —"

A severance, of course from the United Kingdom, the British Crown —

"— I am sure that Her Majesty and the Imperial Parliament would have sanctioned that severance.... That resolution (on the Executive authority) met with the unanimous assent of the Conference. The desire ... to retain our allegiance to Her Majesty was unanimous. Not a single question was made, that it could, by any possibility, be for the interest —"

Observe the word "interest" again.

"— of the colonies or of any section or portion of them, that there should be a severance of our connection."

Sir John might have made another point: all the provinces soon "to be federally united into One Dominion under the Crown" had always been monarchies — none of them had ever been republics. The tradition of monarchy would continue, but Canada's Crown would be unique.

Below

The Duke and Duchess of Connaught at their installation in the Legislative Council Chamber in Quebec on October 13, 1911. The Duke, son of Queen Victoria, was the first prince of the royal family to become Governor General. Lords Dufferin, Lansdowne, Aberdeen, Minto, Byng, Willingdon and Tweedsmuir were also installed in Quebec.

Above

The Fathers of Confederation at Quebec on October 10, 1864. Their first and unanimous decision was that Canada should continue to be a monarchy.

The British and Canadian Crowns

In Britain, the monarchy was supported by a powerful aristocracy and an established church. The members of a large and active royal family rendered it locally present by visits and acts of patronage. It bound together, as it still does five generations later, a large population living under a single government on a relatively small island. It appealed, as it does to a large extent in our own time, to the Briton's deep sense of tradition and his consciousness of the gradations in rank and title by which, as an individual, he relates to others. In Canada, a large territory with a relatively small and scattered population ruled by one central and several provincial governments, a vast area where social and cultural groups and their relationships vary widely, the notion and reality of the Crown could include none of these ingredients.

The Canadian Crown would manifest itself in several persons. The monarch would wear it by hereditary right and the Governor General would represent it by right of appointment, as would each of the Lieutenant Governors in the provincial jurisdictions. "We provide," declared Sir John,

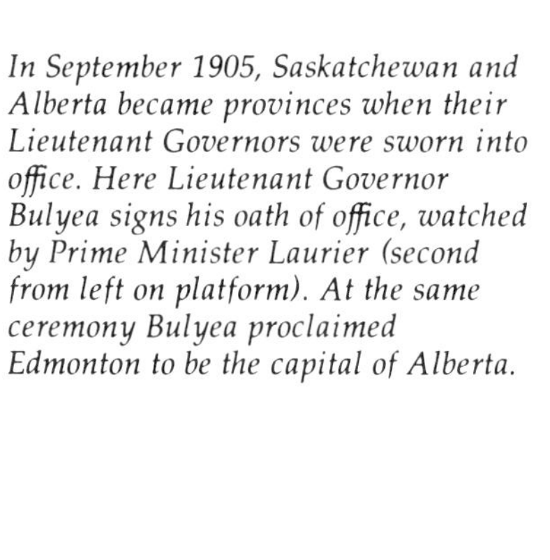

In September 1905, Saskatchewan and Alberta became provinces when their Lieutenant Governors were sworn into office. Here Lieutenant Governor Bulyea signs his oath of office, watched by Prime Minister Laurier (second from left on platform). At the same ceremony Bulyea proclaimed Edmonton to be the capital of Alberta.

that the Executive authority shall be administered by the Sovereign personally or by the representative of the Sovereign duly authorized.... The Executive authority must therefore be administered by Her Majesty's representative.

The British North America Act therefore specifically refers to the separate offices of the representatives of the Crown, in person or in council, and gives them each a number of separate statutory responsibilities. The Queen is referred to seventeen times, the Lieutenant Governors twenty-seven times, and the Governor General thirty-five times. For the first time in history, an historic monarchy, a young parliamentary democracy and a new federal state were reconciled in one political system.

The Governor General

Since 1867, the office of the Governor General has continued to evolve as it did before Confederation. The office has been a faithful mirror of Canada's gradual and peaceful transformation from the status of a Dominion, autonomous and self-governing only in local matters, to that of a fully independent sovereign state.

During the first sixty years after Confederation, the Governor General continued to

Lord Monck opening the first Parliament of the new Dominion of Canada on November 7, 1867. Drawing by Alfred Jones for Harper's Weekly.

exercize varying degrees of political power. In local, purely Canadian matters, he was bound by the convention established in 1848 by Lord Elgin to follow the advice of his prime minister. But in several other areas he represented the British government and was obliged to carry out its policies. In other words, he was at the same time a non-partisan head of state for Canada and an agent of the government of the United Kingdom. It was through his office that communications passed between the Canadian and British administrations, and his appointment was made by the monarch on the recommendation of the British Cabinet in London.

However, as the Canadian Parliament, often with the discreet encouragement of the Governor General, gradually extended its authority, especially in the areas of defence and external affairs, the Governor General's task as a representative of the British government was reduced accordingly. By 1916, Canada was almost completely self-governing. In that year, the prime minister, Sir Robert Borden, formally protested that he had not been consulted when the Duke of Devonshire had been appointed Governor General. Within a decade, the question of Canada's sovereignty was formally raised at the Imperial Conference of

Prime Minister Mackenzie King leaving the Ritz Hotel during the Imperial Conference of 1926. Accompanying him are the Minister of Justice, Ernest Lapointe, and the High Commissioner in Britain, Peter Larkin. In the background, Vincent Massey. At the conference it was agreed that the Canadian Governor General would no longer represent the British government.

1926. (The report of that conference resulted in the Statute of Westminster, which in 1931 established Canada's complete sovereignty.) Henceforth the representatives of the Crown were no longer in any respect entitled to speak for the British government. As the report of the Imperial Conference stated, the Governor General was to hold

> in all essential respects the same position in relation to the administration of public affairs in the dominion as is held by the King in Great Britain ... he is not the representative or agent of His Majesty's government in Great Britain or any Department.... Future recommendations to this office should be a matter for the sovereign on the one side and His Majesty's privy council for Canada on the other.

The Canadian Crown had assumed its full constitutional meaning. The Governor General would follow in all areas of policy the precedents set by Lord Elgin. His appointment would henceforth be made only after consultation with the Canadian government.

In fact, the manner of the Governor General's appointment has also evolved in accordance with the development of Canada's status. After Sir Robert Borden's protest in 1916, the British government regularly consulted the Canadian prime minister in preparing a list of

King George VI and Queen Elizabeth being greeted in Quebec City on May 17, 1939, by Prime Minister Mackenzie King and the Minister of Justice, Ernest Lapointe. They were the first sovereigns to tour Canada.

Below right
Viscount Alexander of Tunis and Lady Alexander were the last British vice-regal couple to live at Rideau Hall. They are seen here in the grand entrance.

Below left
The first Canadian-born Governor General in modern times, Vincent Massey is here greeted by Prime Minister Louis St. Laurent as he arrives for his installation in the Senate chamber in 1952.

names to be submitted to the monarch. Then in 1931, when Lord Bessborough (1931-1935) was appointed, the initiative came from Ottawa. After consulting the British government, Prime Minister R.B. Bennett sent several names to King George V (1910-1936). The King indicated his preference, and the Prime Minister then made a formal recommendation. When the Right Honourable Vincent Massey was appointed in 1952, Prime Minister Louis St. Laurent, after ascertaining King George VI's (1936-1952) pleasure, did not consult anyone outside Canada and submitted a single name to the King.

Viscount Willingdon (1926-1931) was the first Governor General since 1760 to "reign" exclusively as the representative of the King's person. He did not, however, exercise all the King's prerogatives. For another twenty years, a number of matters — in fact, those on which in earlier days the British government had kept responsibility — continued to be referred to the King directly by the Canadian government. Thus, for example, Canada's formal proclamation of war in 1939, the granting of honours and the accrediting of ambassadors and ministers abroad went to the King for his signature rather than to the Governor General.

In 1947, however, King George VI approved the issue of new Letters Patent for the office of Governor General. In these, Viscount Alexander (1946-1952) was expressly authorized and empowered to exercise all the prerogatives, powers and authorities which the King himself held as King of Canada.

Some matters, nevertheless, continued to be submitted to the King, and since 1952, to his daughter, our present Queen Elizabeth. These included the proclamation of the Canadian flag and the Letters Patent creating the Order of Canada and the Order of Military Merit as well as Canadian decorations for bravery. The formal letters accrediting Canadian ambassadors abroad were also regularly signed by the Queen. After her Jubilee visit in 1977, Her Majesty approved the transfer to the Governor General of all these functions, and thus concluded the process that had been initiated in 1947.

The Lieutenant Governors

The Fathers of Confederation were not unanimous in deciding that Lieutenant Governors were to participate fully in provincial aspects

Below
The Badge of a Commander of the Order of Military Merit, an order established in 1972 to recognize exceptional devotion to duty by members of the Canadian armed forces. The Governor General is Chancellor of the Order.

Left
In 1976 Mme Léger became the first wife of a Governor General to share in the reading of the speech from the throne at the opening of Parliament in Ottawa.

of the Crown's sovereignty. At first the majority agreed that the Lieutenant Governor was to be a "federal officer," that is, a representative of the federal government who would act as an intermediary between Ottawa and the provincial administrations. He would have the authority to veto or reserve for the federal government provincial bills which he might not consider to be in the interests of the whole country. The majority of the Fathers therefore decided that he would have tenure of office for at least five years. The federal government would appoint him and pay his salary, and could remove him — as it has done on two occasions. Moreover, they made the office of Lieutenant Governor the only part of the provincial constitution that the legislatures of the provinces could not freely amend.

A minority thought otherwise, most notably Sir Oliver Mowat, who played an important part as a delegate to the Quebec Conference, and who was later to serve as premier of Ontario, minister in the federal cabinet and eventually as Lieutenant Governor of Ontario (1897-1903). Together with some of his colleagues from New Brunswick, he initiated a series of court cases that eventually brought the Judicial Committee of the Privy Council, at

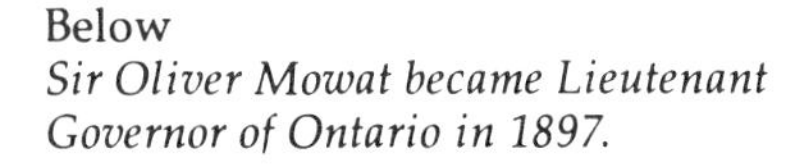

Below
Sir Oliver Mowat became Lieutenant Governor of Ontario in 1897.

Right
Torchlight demonstration at Government House, Fredericton, on Queen Victoria's birthday, 1858. From the Illustrated London News.

the time the highest court of appeal in all British territories, to recognize the Lieutenant Governors as full representatives of the Crown for all purposes of provincial government.

Between the early 1870s and 1892 there was much argument over the question of the role of the Lieutenant Governor. The British North America Act had been ambiguous. On the one hand, it provided for the Lieutenant Governor's appointment by the Governor General and not by Her Majesty. On the other hand, it granted the Lieutenant Governor a great seal, which is the main instrument and symbol of sovereign authority, and it authorized

Above right
The Honourable Francis L. Jobin was appointed Lieutenant Governor of Manitoba in 1976.

Above left
The Honourable Gordon A. Winter became Lieutenant Governor of Newfoundland in 1974.

Left
The Prince of Wales, later Edward VIII, being greeted in St. John's, Newfoundland on August 13, 1919, by Sir Charles Harris, Governor of Newfoundland. The Prince was making a tour of Canada and Newfoundland following the end of World War I.

Below
The Honourable John Elvin Schaffner became Lieutenant Governor of Nova Scotia in 1978. Here he wears the full dress civil uniform traditionally worn by many Lieutenant Governors.

him to act "in the Queen's name." Because of this ambiguity, the prime minister, the colonial secretary and sometimes the Governor General tended to look upon the Lieutenant Governors as subordinate officers. Lord Dufferin, for example, insisted they ought to be addressed as "Your Honour" rather than "Your Excellency." However, the premiers, and eventually the law lords of the Judicial Committee of the Privy Council, gradually became more and more explicit in their opinion of the Lieutenant Governor's role.

In 1883, in the court case of *Hodge* v. *The Queen*, the Judicial Committee of the Privy Council took a significant step toward the recognition of a provincial Crown. This trial revolved around a man named Thomas Hodge who had been fined twenty dollars under an Ontario law for allowing a game of billiards to go on in his Toronto tavern after hours. When the case came to the Judicial Committee, counsel for Hodge argued that Ontario had had no right to pass the Licensing Commission Act of 1877 because it conflicted with the power of the Canada Temperance Act. The Committee upheld Hodge's conviction on the ground that liquor regulation had two aspects: the general power to regulate and the local power to make

Above
The Honourable Jean-Pierre Côté, Lieutenant Governor of Quebec since 1978, arrives in Bagotville to present new colours to Squadron 425.

Above
Hughes Lapointe, Lieutenant Governor of Quebec from 1966 to 1978, accepts the oath of Lise Bacon in his study at the National Assembly in Quebec on November 13, 1973. Premier Bourassa looks on. The representative of the Crown presides at the swearing-in of every cabinet minister.

police regulations and license taverns. This "aspect doctrine" held that each of the governments could, in a sense, be "sovereign." The judgement referred to section 92 of the British North America Act, which enumerates the exclusive powers of provincial legislatures, and stated that "within these limits of subject and area, the local legislature is supreme and has the same authority as the imperial parliament or the parliament of the dominion."

Finally the Judicial Committee definitely settled the issue in 1892, in the case of the *Liquidators of the Maritime Bank of Canada* v. *The Receiver General of New Brunswick*. In this

Far left
A former Chief of the Saddle Lake Indian Band, the Honourable Ralph Steinhauer became Lieutenant Governor of Alberta in 1974. Here he wears Indian regalia to open the Alberta Legislature on February 24, 1977.

Above
The Honourable Gordon Bennett, who was appointed Lieutenant Governor of Prince Edward Island in 1974, presents the award of St. John of Jerusalem to Const. Hall of the RCMP at Charlottetown in August 1977. Lieutenant Governors are Knights of the Order of St. John of Jerusalem; the Governor General is Prior of the Order.

Above
The Honourable C. Irwin McIntosh was appointed Lieutenant Governor of Saskatchewan in February 1978.

case, the Receiver General of the province, on behalf of the New Brunswick government, had deposited 35,000 dollars in the Maritime Bank of Canada. When the bank failed, one of the principal points to be resolved was whether the Province had a right to assets prior to that of other depositors. Its lawyers argued that it did because the Province could claim the prior rights of the Crown. Counsel for the bank stated that the Lieutenant Governor did not represent the Crown and hence the Receiver General could not insist on the Province's priority. The Committee disagreed. Referring to the British North America Act, the judgement stated:

> By section 58, the appointment of a provincial governor is made by the "Governor General in council by instrument under the Great Seal of Canada" or, in other words, by the executive government of the dominion, which is by section 9, expressly declared "to continue and be vested in the Queen." There is no constitutional anomaly in an executive officer of the Crown receiving his appointment at the hands of a governing body who has no powers or functions except as representatives of the Crown; and a Lieutenant Governor, when appointed, is as much the representative of Her Majesty for all purposes of provincial government as the Governor General himself is for all purposes of dominion government.

Below left
The Honourable Hédard Robichaud, first Lieutenant Governor of New Brunswick of Acadian origin, took office in 1971. He is seen here inspecting a guard of honour at the opening of the Legislature in March 1978.

Right
The Honourable Henry P. Bell-Irving was sworn in as Lieutenant Governor of British Columbia on May 18, 1978. Seen here with Mrs. Bell-Irving, he wears the uniform of Honorary Colonel, Seaforth of Canada.

By 1892, therefore, the provincial governments were considered sovereign in their own sphere. The Judicial Committee of the Privy Council had come to share the opinion of those Fathers of Confederation who had sought, with some imagination, to make use of the Crown as the legal and constitutional link between the different parts of Canada.

This adaptation of the Crown to a federal system was a unique and daring experiment. But it works. The sovereignty of the same Crown is exercised by different representatives in different jurisdictions. Thus diversity has been reconciled to unity. Eleven decades after

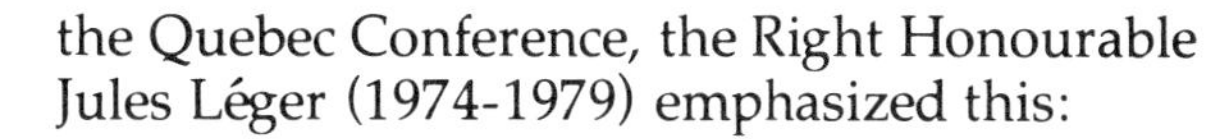

the Quebec Conference, the Right Honourable Jules Léger (1974-1979) emphasized this:

> Down through the centuries, Canadians have evolved a system under the Crown which is well adapted to our country and to our character. This political system is of great value. It has enabled us to develop as a free people and a united people, despite our vast territory and cultural diversity.

Below
Roland Michener presents the Mace to the speaker of the Assembly of the Yukon, March 1972.

Left
The Honourable Pauline McGibbon, Lieutenant Governor of Ontario since 1974, is the first woman to be appointed Lieutenant Governor and the first Canadian woman to be made an Honorary Colonel of a regiment. She wears the uniform of the 25 Toronto Service Battalion.

4
Royal responsibilities

Queen Elizabeth and Prince Philip take the salute from the guard of honour at the Parliament Buildings in October 1957.

In Toronto during the summer of 1973, Queen Elizabeth reminded some 1,400 guests at an official dinner given by the Province of Ontario that "the Crown is an idea more than a person, and I would like the Crown to represent everything that is best and most admired in the Canadian ideal." This representational, or symbolic, role of the Queen, the Governor General and the Lieutenant Governors is probably the best known aspect of their offices. But they have other responsibilities — less visible, but still important parts of the Canadian constitution. These responsibilities can be divided into three areas: prerogative, power and influence.

Vincent Massey opened Parliament on the day of his installation in 1952. Here he takes the royal salute, wearing the traditional Governor General's uniform.

Below right
The Honourable Hédard Robichaud greets the President of Sénégal, Léopold Senghor, on his visit to New Brunswick in June 1976.

Below left
General Vanier accepts the Letters of Credence of the American Ambassador, Livingston T. Merchant, on March 15, 1961. The Governor General receives the Letters of each new Ambassador to Ottawa.

The royal prerogative

Before there was a Parliament, the Crown held a whole bundle of ancient privileges, discretionary powers and traditional rights that belonged to it from its earliest beginnings. There was really no one else to hold these or to exercise them. They were not set down anywhere, but were simply what everyone recognized as part of the responsibility of government. After kings and governors began to summon parliaments, some of these powers were limited or abolished, some fell into disuse, and others were transformed into written laws (statutes). Those that remain with the Crown, and which its representatives can use without the authority of an Act of Parliament, are referred to as "the royal prerogative."

The right to prorogue (discontinue the meeting of) and dissolve the federal Parliament and provincial Legislatures is part of the royal prerogative. So is the right to ownerless property, *le domaine du Roi* or Crown land, and, as has been seen, the right to priority as a creditor in cases of bankruptcy. Other prerogatives are the presiding over the opening of Parliament, the right to make treaties and to receive and send ambassadors, and the main-

tenance of the office of Governor General. Within the provincial jurisdiction, the royal prerogative is held by the Lieutenant Governor. In both jurisdictions it is effected by Orders-in-Council, commissions, proclamations, writs, warrants or Letters Patent issued over the seals of the Queen, the Governor General or the Lieutenant Governor, or over the Great Seals of Canada or the provinces.

Since the time when Lord Elgin and Sir John Harvey bound themselves to follow the "advice" of a first minister in all local matters, and in external affairs since the Imperial Conference of 1926, the exercise of the royal pre-

The present Great Seal of Canada. Designed by Eric Aldwinckle, it shows Queen Elizabeth with the insignia of her coronation, and the royal arms of Canada. Authorized in November 1955, it was entrusted to Vincent Massey on February 25, 1956.

The first Great Seal of Canada following Confederation. It shows Queen Victoria with her coronation regalia, and carries the royal arms and those of the first four provinces of the new Dominion. Documents which carry the Great Seal are recognized as expressing the authority of the sovereign.

Above
The Privy Seal of General Vanier. Certain documents issued under the authority of the Governor General must bear the Governor's personal seal. General Vanier's seal carries his coat of arms, which recalls his French and Irish ancestry, the Royal 22e Régiment, and the Citadel at Quebec.

Below
The Great Seal of the Province of Manitoba, used between 1870 and 1905.

rogative has been all but completely restricted to actions taken on the initiative of the prime minister or premier. There is hardly any prerogative the Crown can invoke without a written form, and since the required seal is in the custody of a minister whose counter-signature must be affixed to the document concerned, there are few matters on which a minister's involvement is not required.

Practically, the royal prerogative provides a convenient mechanism for many important activities of government that would otherwise have no legal basis. Canada, unlike most countries, has a constitution whose provisions are not all dictated by rules set down in writing on a single document. Rather, it is an historic (some say "organic") constitution, made up firstly of customs, conventions, traditions and general (often informal) agreements which remain unwritten, and secondly, of a set of documents, judicial decisions, royal instructions, proclamations and acts of Parliament. The British North America Act of 1867 is, of course, the main constitutional document. But nowhere in its clauses, nor in any other major constitutional record, is there mention of the cabinet, or of the leader of the opposition. Nowhere is there a description of the practice

General Vanier with Queen Elizabeth in 1964 in the Memorial Chapel at the Citadel. General Vanier was buried in this chapel in 1967. When a Governor General dies in office, as General Vanier did, or leaves Canada for more than thirty days, the Chief Justice of the Supreme Court of Canada automatically succeeds him as "Administrator" with all his powers and authorities.

of cabinet or "responsible" government which is the basis of our type of parliamentary democracy. Nowhere is there reference to the prime minister. It is in the royal prerogative that these offices and institutions find their source; from it that the prime minister receives his authority and power.

The royal prerogative is also a subtle control. In a country which has tended to re-elect the same governments several times and with comfortable majorities, the occasional, independent use of certain royal prerogatives by the Crown's representatives may be one of the few constitutional safeguards preventing ministers from becoming too powerful or abusing their authority. In their book *The Constitutional Process in Canada*, Professors R.I. Cheffins and R.N. Tucker have noted how the Crown is a guarantee against abuse:

> To cast aside without question any independent role whatsoever for either the Governor General or the Lieutenant Governors is to remove one of the few — and in many cases, the only — possible restraints on the actions of the prime minister or a provincial premier.
>
> While recognizing that ultimate authority must always rest in some decision-maker, one must at the same time recognize that excessive authority placed in a few hands without recourse to other sources of

His Excellency the Rt. Hon. Edward Schreyer signs his first order-in-council in his study at Rideau Hall after his installation in January 1979.

power is extremely dangerous. In Canada we have perhaps reached this very dangerous position and those persons who have glibly suggested that the Governor General and provincial Lieutenant Governors should be purely ceremonial figures have done the cause of countervailing power a considerable disservice.... It is part of our tradition that these office-holders will almost always act on the advice of their chief advisors at the federal and provincial level. This is the way it is, and this is the way it should be. The Governor General and the Lieutenant Governors are appointees and elected officials should play the predominant role in our governmental and constitutional system. This is not to say, however, that just because these men are appointees they should have no power whatever.

In *The Crown in Canada*, Professor Frank MacKinnon has made the same point vividly:

The offices of Governor General and Lieutenant Governor are constitutional fire extinguishers with a potent mixture of powers for use in great emergencies. Like real extinguishers, they appear in bright colours and are strategically located. But everyone hopes their emergency powers will never be used; the fact they are not used does not render them useless; and it is generally understood there are severe penalties for tampering with them.

The emergency powers of the Crown have developed because serious trouble is inevitable in government and some special apparatus must be kept in reserve ready for use should other safety devices fail.

As this passage of Professor MacKinnon's

Lord and Lady Grey with Sir Wilfrid and Lady Laurier and other dignitaries leaving the memorial services for Edward VII on May 20, 1910.

indicates, most constitutional authorities agree that the royal prerogative still holds an undefinable reserve of power, a special discretionary authority which the representatives of the Crown may use, even independently, in times of emergency or exceptional circumstances. All agree on at least two types of crises when the Crown may be called upon to take direct responsibility. These concern the appointment of a first minister and the dissolution of Parliament.

Appointment of a first minister

The representative of the Crown has the duty to see that the country or province always has a first minister who represents or, as the phrase goes, "has the confidence of" the majority of the elected members of the Legislature. Normally the appointment of this first minister is a routine matter, since political parties choose their leaders. The Governor General or the Lieutenant Governor sends for the leader of the party commanding a majority in the elected house. But should a prime minister or premier die in office (two have in the

The Governor General is responsible for seeing that the country is never without a prime minister. Roland Michener is seen here immediately after swearing in Pierre Trudeau on April 20, 1968.

federal government since Confederation, and a good many in provincial governments) the Crown must find a replacement as soon as possible. Senator Eugene Forsey explains:

> The country cannot wait two or three months for the party in power to choose a new leader. So the Governor General consults leading members of the party (active or retired) to see who is most likely to be able to form a government which will command a majority in the house till the party can choose a new leader. He then calls on the man (or woman) these consultations indicate.
>
> The prime minister so chosen will, of course, hold office only till the party can choose a new leader. If it chooses the prime minister, he remains in office. If it chooses someone else, he gives the place to that person.

There have been few occasions in Canadian history when this situation has presented any difficulty.

Should a first minister resign before his party has chosen a new leader, the Governor General exercises the same responsibility. He may ask the retiring minister for an opinion, but he is not obliged to follow it. In addition, he may consult with the members of the outgoing Cabinet and the leading members of the party in power. Sometimes these may be ready with a recommendation, but occasionally they may tender conflicting advice. The Governor General or the Lieutenant Governor must

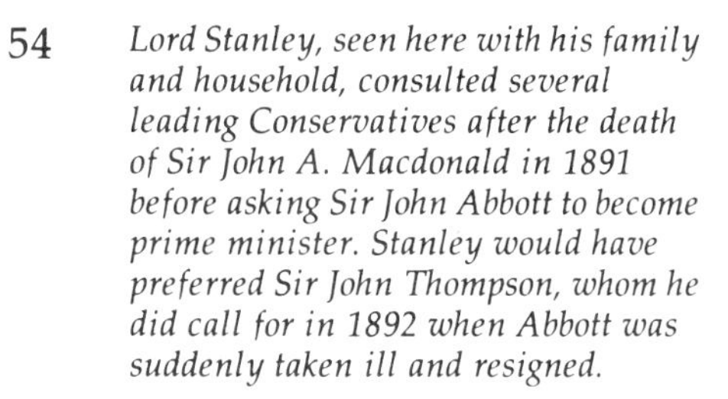

Lord Stanley, seen here with his family and household, consulted several leading Conservatives after the death of Sir John A. Macdonald in 1891 before asking Sir John Abbott to become prime minister. Stanley would have preferred Sir John Thompson, whom he did call for in 1892 when Abbott was suddenly taken ill and resigned.

therefore rely on insight and acumen to summon the person best able to command the majority of the house. Again, the new prime minister or premier will remain in office only so long as he continues to enjoy a majority.

When a prime minister loses his majority, and after the Crown has accepted his resignation, the Governor General or Lieutenant Governor must send for the person able to command the majority. But should a political crisis develop because of doubts over which leader of several parties may be best able to command such support, the representative of the Crown, after consultation with political leaders, must exercise his personal discretion in appointing a first minister. To deny this responsibility would be rash, since the very stability of government may be at stake. Therefore it is in the people's interest that the Crown's prerogative be used to deal with the emergency.

The reverse of the responsibility for appointment is that for dismissal. This prerogative has seldom been exercised in our history, and not since 1903. Lieutenant Governors have dismissed premiers on five occasions — in Quebec in 1878 and 1891, and in British Columbia in 1898, 1900 and 1903. No Governor

Lord Aberdeen is seen here in his robes as a Knight Grand Cross of the Order of St. Michael and St. George. After Sir John Thompson's sudden death in 1893, Lord Aberdeen received conflicting advice from politicians on whom to select as prime minister. He chose Sir Mackenzie Bowell, and on Bowell's resignation in 1896, followed his suggestion to call for Sir Charles Tupper. When the latter's party was defeated in the general election of 1896, Aberdeen refused to follow Tupper's advice to sanction last-minute appointments before asking Wilfrid Laurier to form a government.

General has ever dismissed a federal prime minister. On some occasions, however, the representatives of the Crown seemed ready to use this prerogative. Lieutenant Governor D.C. Cameron of Manitoba (1911-1916) used the threat of dismissal in 1915 to force the premier to institute an impartial royal commission. The commission uncovered enough wrongdoing to bring on the resignation of the government. In 1971, when Premier Smallwood of Newfoundland had lost his majority and seemed reluctant to resign, Frank Moores, then the leader of the opposition, asked that the prerogative be invoked. On that occasion it was not. But it may

Luc Letellier de St. Just (seated), Lieutenant Governor of Quebec from 1876 to 1879, with Henri Joly de Lotbinière, premier of the province. Letellier used the royal prerogative to dismiss the previous premier in 1878 on the grounds that the latter had not respected his "right to be consulted" before presenting a bill dealing with finances to the Legislature. He invited Joly, leader of the opposition, to form a government. Letellier was himself dismissed a year later by the federal government.

sometimes happen that the threat of dismissal is as powerful a tool as the actual exercise of the prerogative.

It would seem that the representatives of the Crown could resort to dismissal when a government flagrantly violated the constitution or was involved in a very serious scandal, if at the same time the members of Parliament and/or the electorate found themselves unable to resist or defeat it. For example, a general election might have reduced a government to a minority. If the prime minister refused to summon Parliament, financing the activities of his administration with Governor General's warrants rather than through a budget approved by Parliament, the representative of the Crown would eventually be obliged to refuse to sign the warrants and insist that Parliament be summoned. Should the prime minister then refuse to advise the summoning of Parliament, the Governor would have cause to dismiss him and call on the leader of the opposition to form a government. About this and other examples, Professor Frank MacKinnon has written:

> The possibility ... is now fortunately remote in Canada. The power can therefore be left in case Canada should have one of those serious upsets experienced elsewhere when a prime minister can take over un-

The Governor General's standard. After it was agreed that the Governor General would no longer represent the British Government, a personal standard was designed for the office. First flown by Lord Bessborough in 1931, it has since continually accompanied the Governor General to indicate his presence.

hindered control of the Constitution as well as of the government. The power is safe where it is, as a deterrent to the prime minister who is not likely to provoke it, and as an ultimate weapon for the governor who is in no position to use it without the most extreme provocation.

Dissolution of Parliament

The second instance in which the representatives of the Crown still retain personal discretion is in the dissolution of Parliament. Many authorities agree that the Queen, the Governor General and the Lieutenant Governors can no longer force an unwilling prime minister to recommend a dissolution of Parliament. But some, notably Senator Forsey, consider that in some circumstances, for example if a government won an election by means of flagrant corruption, fraud, or terrorism, the representative of the Crown might properly dismiss the first minister and call to office a new government to hold new elections. There are no precedents in recent Canadian or British history for this. But in the reverse situation, must the Crown always accept the prime minister's "advice" to dissolve Parliament and call a general election? Based on the principle that the will of the people democratically expressed in

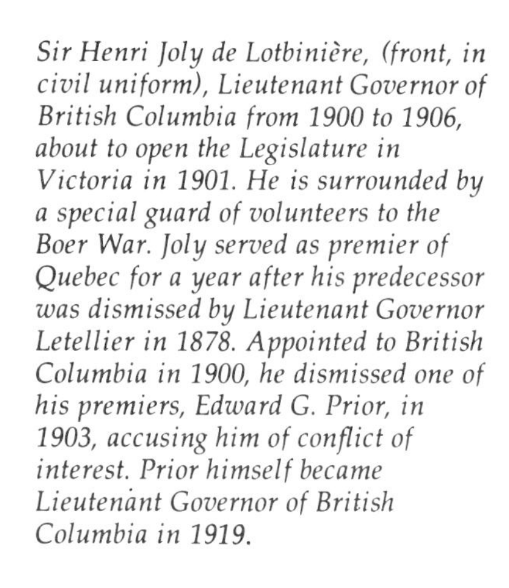

Sir Henri Joly de Lotbinière, (front, in civil uniform), Lieutenant Governor of British Columbia from 1900 to 1906, about to open the Legislature in Victoria in 1901. He is surrounded by a special guard of volunteers to the Boer War. Joly served as premier of Quebec for a year after his predecessor was dismissed by Lieutenant Governor Letellier in 1878. Appointed to British Columbia in 1900, he dismissed one of his premiers, Edward G. Prior, in 1903, accusing him of conflict of interest. Prior himself became Lieutenant Governor of British Columbia in 1919.

an election must be respected, experts would answer in the negative.

Examples will illustrate. If, as Prime Minister Mackenzie King suggested that he might in 1925, a prime minister advised a dissolution immediately after losing an election and before Parliament was able to meet, the Governor General could refuse, indeed should refuse. His responsibility is to give Parliament a chance to meet and express itself. Again, if a government was defeated on a motion of want of confidence within the first few days of a newly elected Parliament, and if a prime minister asked for a dissolution when the leader of the opposition was ready to form a government, the representative of the Crown could quite properly refuse. Senator Forsey has given a good example that is not too far from that case:

> Suppose the Government gets a dissolution, and no one gets a clear majority. The government retains office and meets the new parliament (as it has a perfect right to do), hoping to pick up enough votes from the third party to keep it in power. But the new parliament defeats it. It declines to resign (governments don't resign automatically on defeat). Instead it asks for a second dissolution, and upon a further defeat in the ensuing parliament, a third, and so on, till the electors give in or revolt. Is the Governor General bound to acquiesce in this game of constitutional ping-pong: from

electorate to parliament, from parliament to electorate again, back and forth interminably?

The answer is obviously no. On the other hand, the political situation and circumstances might suggest another course to the representative of the Crown. Therefore much will depend on the Governor's wisdom and discretion, and on his finding an alternative first minister who is able to command the confidence of the House. In the first and only Canadian instance when a dissolution was refused, in 1926, it is still a matter of debate among constitutional authorities whether or not the Governor General, Lord Byng (1921-1926), had actually been able to find such a leader. Prime Minister Arthur Meighen, who was called upon to form a government to replace that of Mackenzie King (who had resigned), won a majority four times in the House. But he was himself forced to advise a dissolution a few days later after losing (by one vote) a motion declaring his ministry unconstitutional. As for Prime Minister King's original "advice" to the Governor General, most constitutional experts agree that because there was a motion censuring King's administration before the House when he tendered it, Lord Byng followed the proper course in refusing to dissolve.

General the Baron Byng of Vimy, seen here reviewing a Scout troop on Parliament Hill in 1921, had commanded Canadian forces at Vimy in World War I. The constitutional crisis he became involved in as Governor General was sometimes known as "The King-Byng Thing."

The Queen, the Governor General and the Lieutenant Governors are the custodians of the constitution. Their responsibility is to see that the rules are followed, both the written and the unwritten. This is why they hold the royal prerogative. This is also why they are given a number of powers.

The statutory powers of the Crown

Our democratic system has vested many powers in the Crown. In fact, most laws which are passed either confirm powers already held by the representatives of the Crown, or give them new ones. These are called "statutory powers." But as we have seen, they are not meant to be used personally by the Crown's representatives. They are really for the government. The Queen, the Governor General and the Lieutenant Governors do not usually on their own initiative make appointments or allocate funds for special purposes. Their power is discharged "on the advice" of "responsible" ministers. In fact, most federal and provincial laws use the term Governor General-in-Council or Lieutenant Governor-in-Council to

Jules Léger awarding the Cross of Valour to Mary Dohey, the first living person to receive the award, on December 1, 1975. The award was instituted in 1972 to recognize acts of outstanding heroism. The Governor General, who is responsible for the administration of the Canadian System of Honours, presides at every presentation.

indicate how the power is actually exercised.

When federal or provincial legislation vests such authority specifically in the Governor General or Lieutenant Governor, their power is quite distinct from the Queen's. It does not come from the royal prerogative, but is conferred by Parliament or the Legislatures. As their power is necessary to the continuous functioning of the government, His Excellency and Their Honours remain in office even when the Queen is present in Canada. They continue at all times to discharge their power "on advice."

There are some actions which the representatives of the Crown can and do take on their own. They can appoint their secretary and the officers of their household, decide on whom to bestow the Governor General's medal or other personal decorations and make their own schedule for official visits throughout the country or province. To an extent, too, they may choose from among the many benevolent institutions proposed for their patronage those they wish to promote. But are they free to intervene personally in government? And in what circumstances?

All constitutional authorities share the opinion that it would only be in the most ex-

Right
The Chain of the Chancellor of the Order of Canada, worn by the Governor General by virtue of his office. The Order of Canada was created in 1967 to recognize Canadians who have performed outstanding services.

Far right
The Badge of the Companion of the Order of Canada, worn by the Governor General as Principal Companion. The badge, designed by Bruce Beatty, represents a stylized snowflake.

ceptional circumstances that those exercising the functions of head of state could intervene personally. Still, on some occasions they have. Although no sovereign of Canada has ever exercised the power to withhold assent to a bill, nor any Governor General since Lord Elgin's time, Lieutenant Governors have done so on twenty-eight occasions since 1867, the most recent being in Prince Edward Island in 1945. In his *Memorandum on the Office of Lieutenant Governor of a Province*, J.M. Hendry has this comment:

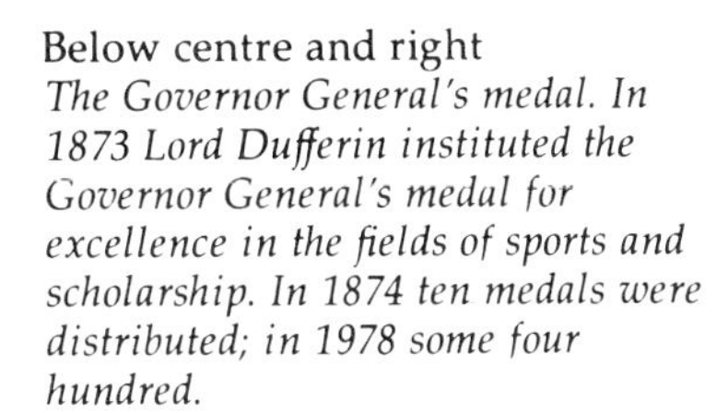

Below centre and right
The Governor General's medal. In 1873 Lord Dufferin instituted the Governor General's medal for excellence in the fields of sports and scholarship. In 1874 ten medals were distributed; in 1978 some four hundred.

The medal awarded by Jules Léger was designed by Alex Colville. The obverse (below centre) carries the profiles of M. and Mme Léger, the reverse (below right), an owl of wisdom hovering over the Crown and maple leaf.

Left
In June 1964, at Rideau Hall, General Vanier inaugurated the Canadian Conference on the Family, which led to the founding of the Vanier Institute.

> The act of a Lieutenant Governor in withholding the assent of the Crown to a bill that has been passed by the legislative chambers ... is a difficult and delicate proceeding. It is one that must obviously be advised by some minister who is in a position to become responsible for the same. If a Lieutenant Governor should for any reason deem it imperative upon him to take such a course, and his ministers should not concur therein, he must be prepared to accept their resignation, and be able to form a new ministry....

In fact, as early as 1882 an order of the Governor General-in-Council advised Lieutenant Governors that the personal, independent use of this power was considered to be obsolete and practically nonexistent.

After the Imperial Conference of 1926 the power granted to the Governor General in section 55 of the British North America Act to reserve bills "for the Queen's pleasure" was declared to be obsolete. In any event it had not been used since 1886. The parallel power granted to Lieutenant Governors to reserve bills for the Governor General's pleasure has not been discarded, however. It has been exercised seventy-one times, the last being in 1961 by the Honourable F.L. Bastedo (1958-1963) of Saskatchewan. However, practice and public pronouncements by provincial and federal politicians indicate that it ought not to be

Below left
In the greenhouse at Rideau Hall Mme Vanier and "Timmy" launch the Easter Seal Campaign.

Below right
Rideau Hall, like many other homes, is visited by young people celebrating Hallowe'en. Here, in the long drawing room of the residence, Mme Léger contributes to the UNICEF *campaign.*

exercised unless the Lieutenant Governor first consults the federal government.

The existence of the royal prerogative and the statutory powers of the Crown as part of the constitution help to ensure good government. However, as exercised independently by the representatives of the Crown, many of these powers and prerogatives are only applicable in rare and extreme situations. In normal circumstances, the Queen, the Governor General and the Lieutenant Governors operate in close accord with the head of the democratically elected majority in Parliament. As a result, it is the Crown's influence that usually plays the more important part in the actual development of government policies.

The influence of the Crown

While the Fathers of Confederation were establishing our government, the English constitutional expert Walter Bagehot was busy writing his *British Constitution*, published in 1867. His chapter on the Crown discussed the distinction between the Crown's powers and influence. As a student preparing for an examination, the young prince who was one day

Below left
F.L. Bastedo, Lieutenant Governor of Saskatchewan, about to open the Legislature in February 1961. It was during this session that he reserved for the Governor General's pleasure the Mineral Contracts Alterations Act.

Below right
As Prince of Wales, the future King George V attended the tercentenary celebrations of Quebec in 1908, two years before he succeeded to the throne. The main ceremony took place at the foot of the Champlain Monument in the old capital.

to become King George V made an abstract of Bagehot's chapter on the Crown. It is so faithful a summary that it can serve here to help define the influence of the monarchy. Prince George wrote:

The Crown is no longer an "Estate of the Realm" or itself the executive, but the Queen nevertheless retains an immense unexhausted *influence* which goes some way to compensate for the formal *powers* which have been lost; this influence can be exercised in various ways:

a) In the *formation* of Ministries; especially in choosing between the Statesmen who have a claim to lead party.

b) During the *continuance* of ministries. The Crown possesses *first* the right to be consulted, *second*, the right to encourage and *third* the right to warn. And these rights may lead to a very important influence on the course of politics....

In Canada, as we have seen, convention has determined that the Crown has little choice in selecting a prime minister from among several leading members of the majority party when this party has an elected leader. However, there is no doubt that the right of the Queen, the Governor General and the Lieutenant Governors to exercise influence remains vested in the Crown. As late as January

Jules Léger poses with Prime Minister Trudeau and members of the cabinet after a cabinet shuffle. Before taking office, all cabinet ministers must be summoned to the Privy Council by the Governor General.

14, 1974, when welcoming the Right Honourable Jules Léger to Ottawa, Prime Minister Trudeau reiterated:

> In his classical work on the English constitution, Walter Bagehot defined the position of the Crown in the following words: "The Sovereign has three rights: the right to be consulted, the right to encourage and the right to warn, and a King of great sense and sagacity would want no others." I hope you will exercise these rights fully.

History and the official biographies or memoirs of the former Governors General and prime ministers have sometimes related the more successful and sometimes the more difficult ways in which these rights have been exercised. Essentially, however, the extent of their use depends on the interpersonal relations between the representatives of the Crown and their first ministers. Many exciting exchanges occurred when the Governor General still acted as the agent of the government of the United Kingdom and when the Lieutenant Governor fully exercised his role as a federal officer. More recently, the Crown's influence has been shown to be of great value when the Governor General or the Lieutenant Governor has been consulted in his capacity as constitutional head of state.

During World War I, the Duke of Connaught took his title as Commander-in-Chief very seriously. He is seen here, with Sir Robert Borden, reviewing troops on Parliament Hill.

Nonetheless, history and memoirs do not reveal everything. On many issues no records are available. And in any event the conversations between the Crown and first ministers remain veiled in strict confidentiality. It is therefore not at all easy to discover exactly how the influence of the Crown's representatives actually operates.

Yet it does operate. The Governor General is informed on the progress of policy and legislation by the regular reception of cabinet minutes and documents, and by visits from the prime minister and other officials. The value of his encouragement and warnings is attested to by many direct and indirect references. Lord Bessborough received so many telephone calls from Prime Minister R.B. Bennett that when the Governor was away from Ottawa and the telephone, his aides noticed how uneasy he became. The present Lieutenant Governor of Ontario, the Honourable Pauline McGibbon, has publicly declared:

> In this Province, the Premier has agreed that if there is a very controversial Bill before the House, that either the minister or deputy minister will come and discuss it with me. I made it clear that I did not wish to obtain my information from the media and he agreed with me.

In a 1977 CBC documentary about the

Below right
Lord Bessborough in 1932 in his study at Rideau Hall inaugurating the Trans Canada telephone service by speaking with each of the Lieutenant Governors.

Below left
The Honourable C. Irwin McIntosh looks on as his premier, Allan Blakeney, signs a petition for Canadian unity.

Canadian monarchy, Prime Minister Trudeau stated that his regular visits to Rideau Hall were "more than courtesy calls on His Excellency." Earlier, in January 1974, when speaking at a banquet in honour of the Right Honourable Roland Michener (1967-1974), he declared, "I recall with personal gratitude the many Wednesday nights since 1968 when you have offered me your encouragement and counsel on the nation's business." Many years before, Prime Minister Sir Robert Borden used almost identical language. "It would be an absolute mistake," he wrote,

> to regard the Governor General as a mere figurehead, a mere rubber stamp. During nine years of Premiership I had the opportunity of realizing how helpful may be the advice and counsel of a Governor General in matters of delicacy and difficulty; in no case was consultation with regard to such matters ever withheld; and in many instances I obtained no little advantage and assistance therefrom.

The Right Honourable Vincent Massey, who was consulted for over seven and a half years by Prime Ministers St. Laurent and Diefenbaker, discussed his role in similar terms in an exchange with journalist Peter Newman:

Below left
Roland Michener and Pierre Trudeau, 1968.

Below right
Vincent Massey, General Vanier and Lord Alexander at a meeting of the Montreal Men's Press Club in 1961.

MASSEY: ... We have someone in the person of the Sovereign who is above all controversy, completely dispassionate, and represents the people as the prime minister represents the government.

NEWMAN: In that context, would you say something about the importance of the Governor Generalship?

MASSEY: I found that the office of Governor General was very misunderstood when I first went to Ottawa. The phrase rubber stamp was used. It's no rubber stamp. The Governor General's views are solicited by the prime minister frequently and he's encouraged to state them. Decisions are made, of course, by the government, not by him.

NEWMAN: But surely you permanently changed the nature of the office because you were a Canadian.

MASSEY: It made a difference I think. It's a very intimate relationship between the two men, the prime minister and the Governor General. Each has his function to perform and they meet and discuss matters confidentially whenever it occurs to either of them to do so. Another thing about the Governor General, he knows more about what's going on than anybody else by virtue of his office.

The representatives of the Crown are indeed among the best informed people in the country. Through travel and hospitality they meet Canadians from every social group and region. In the last quarter century, Queen Elizabeth, the Governor General and the Lieutenant Governors have journeyed to every

Below left
Lord Byng (second from left) inspecting an oil well at Norman Wells, N.W.T., in 1925.

Above
Vincent Massey visiting a mine. Mr. Massey travelled over 200,000 miles across Canada during his term of office.

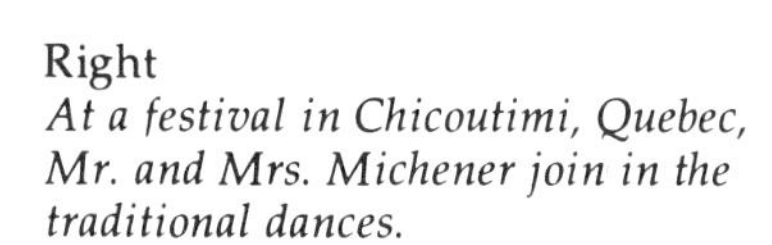

Right
At a festival in Chicoutimi, Quebec, Mr. and Mrs. Michener join in the traditional dances.

part of our country. Altogether they have travelled well over a million miles. In his five year term, for example, the Right Honourable Jules Léger and his wife undertook one hundred tours out of Ottawa.

The Crown's representatives have visited the outposts of Newfoundland, the Yukon and northern Ontario as well as the inner city. They have ascended mountains and descended deep into coal mines. They have attended church services and sporting events, funerals and county fairs, concerts, picnics and centennial celebrations. And they have gone in person to see Canadians in hospitals, senior citizens' homes, housing projects, youth clubs and factories. Thus they have come into personal contact with many people and with a wide variety of opinions.

The hospitality which the representatives of the Crown have extended so liberally at each of their official residences has also developed their relationships with many Canadians. Recalling his years at Rideau Hall and at the Citadel in Quebec, Mr. Michener summed it up in this way:

Our clientele was unlimited — parliamentarians and government officials, foreign and Canadian diplomats

Below right

The Citadel at Quebec has served as the second official residence of the Governor General since 1872. Every Governor General since Lord Dufferin has spent some time there each year.

Above

George Porteous, Lieutenant Governor of Saskatchewan from 1976 to 1977, visits a senior citizens' residence in Saskatchewan in 1977.

(coming and going), the armed forces and military associations, distinguished visitors, domestic and foreign groups of many kinds, Canadian citizens in all their variety, visiting students and children, etc. The events ranged from receiving the letter of an ambassador, to entertaining seven thousand schoolchildren of the Ottawa district at an annual garden party on July 1st.

In fact, during the first two years of his term, Mr. Michener conversed with over three thousand people from every walk of life for at least half an hour. During the next five years, he maintained the same average of about five such visitors a day. Mr. Léger averaged an even higher number of such conversations. In a typical week in the spring of 1976, for instance, he personally received, in addition to the prime minister, the president of a university and that of a school commission, a writer, a popular singer, two directors of Crown agencies, an area commissioner of the Girl Guides, two ambassadors, the leader of a labour union, a newspaperman, the head of an ambulance brigade, three privy councillors and the premier of a province. In that same week he held an investiture of the Order of Canada, welcomed a gathering of school safety patrollers and a group of children participating in Brotherhood Week, and met delegations of Canadian citizen court judges and

Mme Vanier at a children's Christmas party in the Tent Room at Rideau Hall. All Governors General regularly visit schools and receive children at their residences.

parliamentarians from Venezuela.

As a result of their familiarity with the country and the people, the representatives of the Crown are the most accurate, personal, non-partisan barometers of public opinion that a government and its people could wish to have.

Thus, under today's constitution, the influence brought to bear by the representatives of the Crown through the exercise of their right to be consulted, their right to encourage and their right to warn is more regularly significant than their prerogatives and powers. Certainly it is more frequently referred to. Whenever it is, whether it be by politicians or by scholars, it is similarly assessed, as we see in this passage from Professor James Mallory:

> ... the right of the head of state to be fully informed has had a salutary effect on the practice of Cabinet government in Canada.... Decisions are made necessarily by responsible politicians. But when these decisions have to be approved, before being made public, by a personage who is outside the circle of ministers, there is time not only for sober second thought but also for looking at the decision as more than a partisan move.... The institution of constitutional monarchy, by creating a centre of influence (though not of power) at the heart of the decision making process, is a necessary, though necessarily frail, admixture of a non party point of

Jules Léger was a newspaperman in Ottawa in 1938. Shortly after taking office, he visited the press room at Le Droit.

view at the summit. The political system is likely to throw up as its leaders men of strong character. Humility is rare in such men. Their strength lies in their confidence that they represent the right and only course. It is useful that they must make this feeling known to an "outsider." They are thus less likely to confuse an outrageously partisan stroke with the national interest.

74 *Rideau Hall has been the official residence of the Governor General since 1864. The west front, in Renaissance style, was completed in 1913. The coat-of-arms is said to be the largest in the world.*

5
A symbol of our community

As well as being a part of our government, the Crown is also a symbol. The Queen, the Governor General and the Lieutenant Governors continually create and enrich the Canadian heritage. They each represent the country with equal validity, though in different ways. Still, in their symbolic roles, they cannot be separated one from the other. They form a single corporate institution. The governor generalcy and the office of Lieutenant Governor would have much less meaning if they were divorced from the prestige of the sovereign and, in our own day, from the extraordinary mystique of the personal popularity of Queen Elizabeth II.

Above
King George VI and Queen Elizabeth with Lord and Lady Tweedsmuir at Rideau Hall, 1939.

Above
Vincent Massey was a long-time friend of the Royal Family. Here he walks with Her Majesty and Prince Philip through the grounds of Rideau Hall.

Top
When the Queen is in Canada the Governor General acts as her official host. Here she sits with Roland Michener at a banquet at Government House, Victoria, in 1971.

Conversely, the sovereign's responsibility depends upon the actions of the other representatives of the Crown. Through their offices the Canadian monarchy is rendered influential, and through their persons it is made visible among us.

A public appearance by a representative of the Crown has a special meaning. It lends a sense of occasion to any circumstance or event, whether it be the full pageantry of the opening of Parliament or of the Olympic Games, a visit to a camp for crippled children, the inauguration of a new unit of the Red Cross, or the dedication of a public building. Unlike a visit from an elected representative who might be suspected of partisanship or from a famous actor or athlete who could be there to encourage admirers, the attendance of the Crown's representative is a gracious act — a gesture that asks for no return. It is a statement that the event is one which deserves wide attention, an encouragement to many, a sign that the whole province or country appreciates the merits of all those whose work and devotion made it possible.

Such visits also lend colour. As a symbol, the Crown speaks to the imagination and the emotions. It appeals to the senses through

Above
Lord Grey at the unveiling of the Victoria monument in Hamilton, Ontario.

Right
Queen Elizabeth, accompanied by Jules Léger, opens the games of the Twenty-first Olympiad in Montreal on July 17, 1976.

ceremonies which vary extensively according to circumstance and place, but which always include some rite or symbolic act which will lift the moment out of the ordinary. It may be a guard of honour, a mounted escort, or the Crown's standard. It may be the aiguillettes of the aides-de-camp, or the plumes and gold braid of a full dress uniform. It may be the royal salute. Whatever the ritual, it reminds all those who are present of a reality that is greater than each one of them, of the community symbolized by the representatives of the Crown.

Our representatives also give the Canadian Crown much of its engaging originality. Through the successive appointments to the offices of Governor General and Lieutenant Governor, these two institutions draw attention to the aspirations and concerns of Canada's various ethnic, social and regional groups. At the same time they enrich the symbolism of our Crown by associating it with differing creeds, races and ways of life. The Canadian Crown thus becomes both the product and the symbol of the contributions of Canadians from many backgrounds: the literary, the philanthropic, the artistic, the agricultural, the military and the diplomatic.

Above

The Honourable Gordon Winter pays tribute to the war dead in the annual July 1st ceremony at the Cenotaph in St. John's.

Above

The Honourable Pauline McGibbon laying the corner stone of the Rotary-Laughlin Centre in Toronto in 1976. Before her appointment, Mrs. McGibbon was involved in much volunteer work.

Top

The Crown is the "Defender of the Faith" of all Canadians, although there is no established church in Canada. Its representatives regularly attend church services. Here General Vanier enters a synagogue in Ottawa.

The office of Governor General historically embraces, among many other qualities, the excitement and magnificence of Frontenac's explorations and gallantry; the chivalry and altruism of Montmagny (1635-1648), whose association with the care of the sick and injured has been continued, through the Priory of the Order of St. John of Jerusalem, by all the Governors General of modern times, and the interest in athletics of Lord Stanley (1888-1893) and Earl Grey whose trophies have provided hundred of hours of pleasure to millions of Canadians. The royal patronage of Princess Louise, of the Duke of Connaught (1911-1916), and of Princess Alice, and the tradition of study and scholarship encouraged by the examples of Sir Edmund Head (1854-1861) and Lord Lorne, and stimulated further by the Governor General's Literary Awards initiated by Lord Tweedsmuir (1935-1940), are also a part of the position.

Since 1952, when the office was occupied for the first time in the modern era by a native-born Canadian, it has developed even more. The Right Honourable Vincent Massey's important contribution to the arts and his concern for the development of the Canadian identity; General Vanier's (1959-1967) gentle

Above
The Earl of Minto.

Top
John Buchan, first Baron Tweedsmuir of Elsfield.

The Stanley Cup was donated as an award for competition in hockey by Sir Frederick Stanley, Baron Stanley of Preston, in 1893.

Right
Donated by Lord Minto in 1901, the Minto Cup is given to the Canadian Junior Lacrosse Champions.

and abiding religious commitment as well as his interest in family life; Mr. Michener's great appreciation for Parliament and his emphasis on youth and sports; the strength of spirit displayed by Mr. Léger, and his unfailing optimism for the future of Canada; all these have given vitality and meaning to the office. His Excellency the Right Honourable Edward Schreyer has a life-long awareness of the meaning of multiculturalism, and of multilingualism as well. His term will bring to the attention of all Canadians the strength and value of our cultural mosaic.

The office of Governor General is similar

Roland Michener practising for the Grey Cup kick-off, November 1972. Mr. Michener maintained his interest in sports throughout his term as Governor General.

Left
Lord Grey's best-known legacy is the Grey Cup.

to very few others in the world — one of which we can be proud. The same may be said about the offices of the ten Lieutenant Governors. Each has its own local, traditional, evolving character, each is steeped in the history of its own province and each is the product of important concerns.

These representatives of the Crown serve us as official non-partisan hosts to all visiting heads of state and distinguished guests. They receive ambassadors and high commissioners from abroad, and in their official residences they welcome thousands of their fellow citizens who come as part of delegations or as individual guests. In addition, since Lord Willingdon's time the Governor General has travelled abroad to pay our respects to friendly nations. Lieutenant Governors have also represented their provinces within Canada and at times even in other countries.

The Canadian Crown, defined by a long evolution and by the continual action and reaction of Canadians, is distinctly our own. As the annalist of the Ursuline convent in Quebec wrote about Philippe de Vaudreuil (1703-1725), "For twenty-two years, the farmer, the businessman and the soldier alike could only bless his name"; or as former Premier Ross

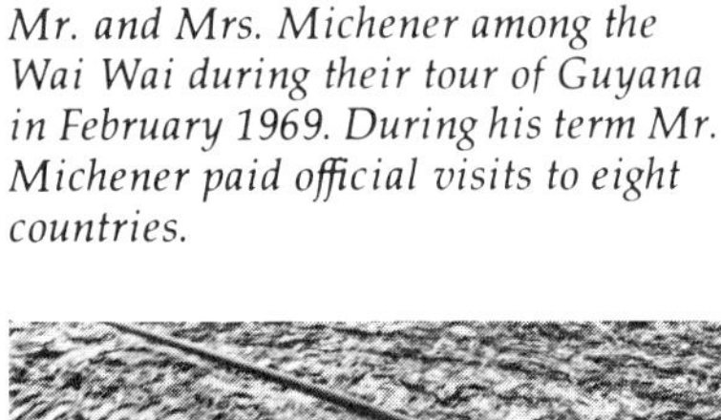

Below
Mr. and Mrs. Michener among the Wai Wai during their tour of Guyana in February 1969. During his term Mr. Michener paid official visits to eight countries.

Above
Lord Athlone conducting General Charles de Gaulle to the War Memorial in Ottawa on July 11, 1944. Canada was one of the first countries to recognize General de Gaulle as a head of state.

Above
The Prime Minister of India, Pandit Nehru (right), was one of the many heads of government received by Vincent Massey during his term of office. Seen here with them is Caroline Massey, Vincent Massey's granddaughter.

Thatcher declared about Lieutenant Governor R.L. Hanbidge (1963-1970) of Saskatchewan, "No one ever found his door closed, his heart empty, or his friendly ear uncooperative." Our governors have been successful, with remarkably few exceptions, in living up to the qualities used by Bishop Briand of Quebec to describe General Murray: "He was moderate, just, humane, tender and compassionate toward the poor and the unfortunate."

A Governor General comes to office not because he is rich, aggressive or powerful, not because he has a wide popular following, nor because he has won an electoral contest. He is

Above
M. and Mme Léger are greeted at the Royal Palace in Madrid by King Juan Carlos of Spain and Queen Sofia in March 1978. Since 1927 Governors General have regularly represented Canada abroad.

Top left
The Honourable F.L. Jobin during an informal moment on his visit in 1976 to the 2nd Battalion, Princess Patricia's Canadian Light Infantry, in Cyprus.

Top right
Philippe de Vaudreuil was appointed in 1703. He was one of the most successful Governors General, and was long remembered by the settlers of New France.

Above right
General James Murray. As the first civil governor after the conquest, Murray developed an admiration for French Canadians whom he termed "perhaps the bravest and the best race upon the Globe."

appointed because of his excellence, because he has proven himself to be dedicated to public service, appreciative of our many cultures, concerned and respectful for the rights of others. Likewise to express the honour of the provinces the Lieutenant Governors are called to their high offices. Therefore, when they act and speak, they do so for all of us.

They stand at the head of our country or province as an affirmation of our brotherhood, of our acceptance of inherited loyalties. They are a subtle presence above our divisions and differences, proving in their very persons and offices that our heritage is a real one. The Queen joins us to an international community, the Lieutenant Governors express our particular local loyalties, and the Governor General reigns *a mari usque ad mare*. Their roles are complex and various in their constitutional and social aspects. But in their essential character they continue Champlain's dream into our own Canadian Elizabethan age. In the long line of those who have represented our country throughout its history, they are living signs of our traditions and of our permanent ideals.

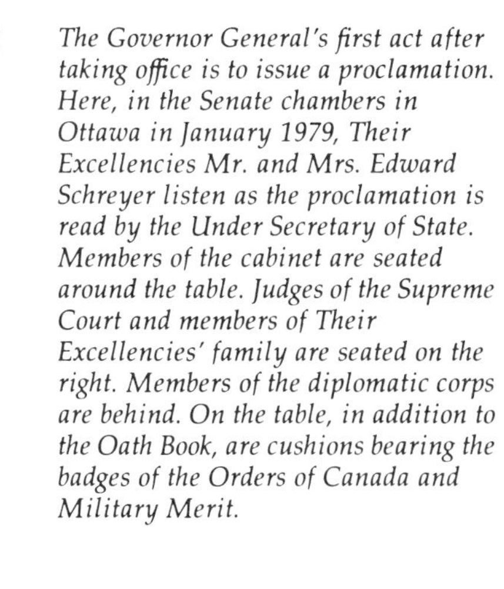

The Governor General's first act after taking office is to issue a proclamation. Here, in the Senate chambers in Ottawa in January 1979, Their Excellencies Mr. and Mrs. Edward Schreyer listen as the proclamation is read by the Under Secretary of State. Members of the cabinet are seated around the table. Judges of the Supreme Court and members of Their Excellencies' family are seated on the right. Members of the diplomatic corps are behind. On the table, in addition to the Oath Book, are cushions bearing the badges of the Orders of Canada and Military Merit.

Sovereigns who have reigned over Canadian territory

(1485)-1509	Henry VII	(1515)-1547	François I
1509-1547	Henry VIII	1547-1559	Henri II
1547-1553	Edward VI	1559-1560	François II
1553-1558	Mary I	1560-1574	Charles IX
1558-1603	Elizabeth I	1574-1589	Henri III
1603-1625	James I	1589-1610	Henri IV
1625-1649	Charles I	1610-1643	Louis XIII
1649-1660	(Republic)	1643-1715	Louis XIV
1660-1685	Charles II	1715-(1775)	Louis XV
1685-1688	James II		
1688-1702	William III		
1688-1694	and Mary II		
1702-1714	Anne		
1714-1727	George I		
1727-1760	George II		
1760-1820	George III		
1820-1830	George IV		
1830-1837	William IV		
1837-1901	Victoria		
1901-1910	Edward VII		
1910-1936	George V		
1936	Edward VIII		
1936-1952	George VI		
1952-	Elizabeth II		

Governors of Canada

This list is limited to those governors who in an unbroken line received commissions from the sovereign as senior representatives of royal authority over the ever-widening territories that now comprise Canada. The dates are those of their assumption and relinquishing of office. The list does not include Administrators. Because their jurisdiction was limited and the line of succession was broken several times, or, for the earlier periods, was difficult to establish, the list also does not include governors of Newfoundland or Acadia, many of whom held royal commissions. Nor does it include the governors of the territories of the Hudson's Bay Company. Their line of succession was also broken on occasion, and, in any event, their appointments were made by the Company, and not by the Crown.

1627-1635	Samuel de Champlain
1635-1648	Charles de Montmagny
1648-1651	Louis d'Ailleboust de Coulonge
1651-1657	Jean de Lauzon
1658-1661	Le vicomte d'Argenson
1661-1663	Le baron d'Avaugour
1663-1665	Augustin de Mésy
1665-1672	Daniel de Courcelle
1672-1682, 1689-1698	Le comte de Frontenac
1682-1685	Joseph-Antoine de LaBarre
1685-1689	Le marquis de Denonville
1698-1703	Hector de Callière
1703-1725	Philippe de Vaudreuil
1726-1747	Le marquis de Beauharnois
1747-1749	Le comte de La Galissonnière
1749-1752	Le marquis de La Jonquière
1752-1755	Le marquis de Duquesne
1755-1760	Pierre de Vaudreuil
1760-1763	Jeffrey Amherst
1764-1768	James Murray
1768-1778, 1786-1796	Sir Guy Carleton, Lord Dorchester
1778-1786	Frederick Haldimand
1796-1807	Robert Prescott
1807-1811	Sir James Craig
1812-1815	Sir George Prevost
1816-1818	Sir John Sherbrooke
1818-1819	The Duke of Richmond
1820-1828	The Earl of Dalhousie
1830-1835	Lord Aylmer
1835-1838	The Earl of Gosford
1838	The Earl of Durham
1838-1839	Sir John Colborne
1839-1841	Lord Sydenham
1842-1843	Sir Charles Bagot
1843-1845	Lord Metcalfe
1845-1847	The Earl Cathcart
1847-1854	The Earl of Elgin
1854-1861	Sir Edmund Head
1861-1868	Viscount Monck
1868-1872	Lord Lisgar
1872-1878	The Earl of Dufferin
1878-1883	The Marquess of Lorne
1883-1888	The Marquess of Lansdowne
1888-1893	Lord Stanley
1893-1898	The Earl of Aberdeen
1898-1904	The Earl of Minto
1904-1911	The Earl Grey
1911-1916	Prince Arthur, Duke of Connaught
1916-1921	The Duke of Devonshire
1921-1926	Lord Byng
1926-1931	Viscount Willingdon
1931-1935	The Earl of Bessborough
1935-1940	Lord Tweedsmuir
1940-1946	The Earl of Athlone
1946-1952	Viscount Alexander
1952-1959	Vincent Massey
1959-1967	Georges-Philéas Vanier
1967-1974	Roland Michener
1974-1979	Jules Léger
1979-	Edward Schreyer

Governors and Lieutenant Governors of Canada's provinces

This list includes those governors who held royal commissions as representatives of either the French or the British Crown. Occasionally both Crowns were represented simultaneously. Some were subordinate to a senior governor, while others held jurisdiction over a limited area. The provinces are listed in their official order, based on their date of entry into Confederation.

Ontario (previously Upper Canada) 1867

1792-1796	Col. John Graves Simcoe
1799-1805	Peter Hunter
1806-1817	Francis Gore
1818-1828	Sir Perigrine Maitland
1828-1836	Sir John Colborne
1836-1838	Sir Francis Bond Head
1838-1841	Sir George Arthur
1867-1868	Sir Henry Stisted
1868-1873	William P. Howland
1873-1875	John Willoughby Crawford
1875-1880	Donald A. Macdonald
1880-1887	John Beverley Robinson
1887-1892	Sir Alexander Campbell
1892-1897	Sir George Kirkpatrick
1897-1903	Sir Oliver Mowat
1903-1908	Sir William Clark
1908-1914	Sir John Gibson
1914-1919	Sir John Hendrie
1919-1921	Lionel Clarke
1921-1927	Henry Cockshutt
1927-1932	William D. Ross
1932-1937	Herbert A. Bruce
1937-1946	Albert Matthews
1946-1952	Ray Lawson
1952-1957	Louis Breithaupt
1957-1963	John Keiller MacKay
1963-1968	William Earl Rowe
1968-1974	W. Ross Macdonald
1974-	Pauline E. McGibbon

Quebec (previously Quebec, Lower Canada) 1867

1766-1768	Sir Guy Carleton
1770-1774	H. Theophilus Cramahé
1784-1785	Henry Hamilton
1785-1786	Henry Hope
1791-1793	Alured Clarke
1796-1797	Robert Prescott
1799-1805	Sir Robert Shore Milnes
1808-1832	Sir Francis Burton
1867-1873	Sir Narcisse Belleau
1873-1876	René Edouard Caron
1876-1879	Luc Letellier de St. Just
1879-1884	Théodore Robitaille
1884-1887	Rodrigue Masson
1887-1892	Sir Auguste Réal Angers
1892-1898	Sir Joseph-Adolphe Chapleau
1898-1908	Sir Louis-Amable Jetté
1908-1911	Sir C.A. Pantaléon Pelletier
1911-1915	Sir François Langelier
1915-1918	Sir E.P.-Evariste Leblanc
1918-1923	Sir Charles Fitzpatrick
1923-1924	Louis-Philippe Brodeur
1924-1929	Narcisse Pérodeau
1929	Sir Lomer Gouin
1929-1934	Henry George Carroll
1934-1939	Esioff-Léon Patenaude
1939-1950	Sir Eugène Fiset
1950-1958	Gaspard Fauteux
1958-1961	Onésime Gagnon
1961-1966	Paul Comtois
1966-1978	Hughes Lapointe
1978-	Jean-Pierre Côté

Nova Scotia (includes Acadia) 1867

1603-1608	Pierre du Gua de Monts
1606-1615	Jean de Poutrincourt
1615 1623	Charles de Biencourt
1631-1642, 1653-1657	Charles de La Tour
1632-1635	Ignace de Razilly
1638-1650	Charles de Menou d'Aulnay
1657-1667	Emmanuel LeBorgne
1662-1667	William Crowne
1657-1670	Thomas Temple
1667-1670	Alexandre LeBorgne de Belle-Isle
1670-1673	Andigné de Grandfontaine

1673-1677	Jacques de Chambly
1684-1687	François-Marie Perrot
1687-1690	Louis-Alexandre des Friches
1691-1700	Joseph-Robineau de Villebon
1701-1705	Jacques-François de Brouillan
1706-1710	Daniel d'Auger de Subercase
1712-1714	Francis Nicholson
1715-1719	Samuel Vetch
1719-1749	Richard Philipps
1749-1752	Edward Cornwallis
1752-1753	Perigrine Hopson
1753-1760	Charles Lawrence
1761-1763	Jonathan Belcher
1763-1766	Montague Wilmot
1766	Michael Francklin
1766-1773	William Campbell
1773-1776	Francis Legge
1776-1778	Marriot Arbuthnot
1778-1781	Sir Richard Hughes
1781-1782	Sir Andrew Hammond
1782-1791	John Parr
1792-1808	Sir John Wentworth
1808-1811	Sir George Prevost
1811-1816	Sir John Sherbrooke
1816-1820	The Earl of Dalhousie
1820-1828	Sir James Kempt
1828-1834	Sir Perigrine Maitland
1834-1840	Sir Colin Campbell
1840-1846	Lord Falkland
1846-1852	Sir John Harvey
1852-1858	Sir John Gaspard Le Marchant
1858-1863	The Earl of Mulgrave
1864-1865	Sir Richard MacDonnell
1865-1867	Sir William Fenwick Williams
1867-1873	Charles Hastings Doyle
1873	Joseph Howe
1873-1883	Adams Archibald
1883-1888	Matthew Henry Richey
1888-1890	Archibald W. McLelan
1890-1900	Malachy B. Daly
1900-1906	Alfred G. Jones
1906-1910	Duncan Campbell Fraser
1910-1915	James D. McGregor
1915-1916	David MacKeen
1916-1925	MacCallum Grant
1925	J.R. Douglas
1925-1930	James Cranswick Tory
1930-1931	Frank Stanfield
1931-1937	W.H. Covert
1937-1940	Robert Irwin
1940-1942	Frederick F. Mathers
1942-1947	Henry Ernest Kendall
1947-1952	J.A.D. McCurdy
1952-1958	Alistair Fraser
1958-1963	Edward Chester Plow
1963-1968	Henry Poole MacKeen
1968-1973	Victor deB Oland
1973-1978	Clarence L. Gosse
1978-	John Elvin Shaffner

New Brunswick 1867

1784-1817	Thomas Carleton
1817-1823	George Strachey Smyth
1824-1831	Sir Howard Douglas
1831-1837	Sir Archibald Campbell
1837-1841	Sir John Harvey
1841-1848	Sir William Colebrooke
1848-1854	Sir Edmund Head
1854-1861	John Manners-Sutton
1861-1866	Arthur Hamilton Gordon
1866-1867	Charles Hastings Doyle
1867-1868	Francis Pym Harding
1868-1873	Lemuel Allan Wilmot
1873-1878, 1885-1893	Sir Samuel Leonard Tilley
1878-1880	Edward B. Chandler
1880-1885	Robert D. Wilmot
1893	John Boyd
1893-1896	John J. Fraser
1896-1902	Abner Ried McClelan
1902-1907	Jabez B. Snowball
1907-1912	Lemuel J. Tweedie
1912-1917	Josiah Wood
1917	Gilbert W. Ganong
1917-1923	William Pugsley
1923-1928	William F. Todd
1928-1935	H.H. McLean
1935-1940	Murray MacLaren
1940-1945	William G. Clark
1945-1958	David L. MacLaren
1958-1965	J. Leonard O'Brien
1965-1968	John B. McNair
1968-1971	Wallace S. Bird
1971-	Hédard Robichaud

Manitoba 1870

1870-1872 Sir Adams Archibald
1872-1877 Alexander Morris
1877-1882 Joseph-Edouard Cauchon
1882-1888 James Cox Aikens
1888-1895 Sir John C. Schultz
1895-1900 James Colebrooke Patterson
1900-1911 Sir Daniel Hunter McMillan
1911-1916 Sir D. Colin Cameron
1916-1926 J.A. Manning Aikens
1926-1929 Theodore Arthur Burrows
1929-1934 James Duncan McGregor
1934-1940 William Johnston Tupper
1940-1953 Roland F. McWilliams
1953-1960 John S. McDiarmid
1960-1965 Erick F. Willis
1965-1970 Richard S. Bowles
1970-1976 William J. McKeag
1976- Francis L. Jobin

British Columbia (including Vancouver Island) 1871

1850-1851 Richard Blanchard
1851-1864 Sir James Douglas
1864-1866 Arthur Edward Kennedy
1864-1869 Frederick Seymour
1869-1871 Sir Anthony Musgrave

1871-1876 Sir Joseph W. Trutch
1876-1881 Albert N. Richards
1881-1887 Clement Francis Cornwall
1887-1892 Hugh Nelson
1892-1897 Edgar Dewdney
1897-1900 Thomas R. McInnes
1900-1906 Sir Henri Joly de Lotbinière
1906-1909 James Dunsmuir
1909-1914 Thomas Wilson Paterson
1914-1919 Sir Frank S. Barnard
1919-1920 Edward G. Prior
1920-1926 Walter Cameron Nichol
1926-1931 Robert Randolph Bruce
1931-1936 J.W.F. Johnson
1936-1941 Eric Werge Hamber
1941-1946 W.C. Woodward
1946-1950 Charles Arthur Banks
1950-1955 Clarence Wallace
1955-1960 Frank Mackenzie Ross
1960-1968 George R. Pearkes
1968-1973 John Robert Nicholson
1973-1978 Walter Stewart Owen
1978- Henry Bell-Irving

Prince Edward Island 1873

1770-1787 Walter Patterson
1787-1805 Edmund Fanning
1805-1812 Joseph Frederick W. DesBarres
1813-1824 Charles D. Smith
1824-1831 John Ready
1831-1835 Sir Aretas Young
1836-1837 Sir John Harvey
1837-1841 Sir Charles Fitzroy
1841-1847 Sir Henry V. Huntley
1847-1850 Sir Donald Campbell
1850-1854 Sir Alexander Bannerman
1854-1859 Sir Dominick Daly
1859-1868 George Dundas
1868-1870 Sir Robert Hodgson
1870-1873 Sir William C.F. Robinson

1874-1879 Sir Robert Hodgson
1879-1884 Thomas H. Haviland
1884-1889 Andrew A. Macdonald
1889-1894 Jedediah S. Carvell
1894-1899 George W. Howlan
1899-1904 Peter A. McIntyre
1904-1910 Donald A. MacKinnon
1910-1915 Benjamin Rogers
1915-1919 Augustine C. Macdonald
1919-1924 Murdoch McKinnon
1924-1930 Frank R. Heartz
1930-1933 Charles Dalton
1933-1939 George de Blois
1939-1945 Bradford W. LePage
1945-1950 Joseph A. Bernard
1950-1958 Thomas W.L. Prowse
1958-1963 F. Walter Hyndman
1963-1969 Willibald J. MacDonald
1969-1974 John George MacKay
1974- Gordon L. Bennett

Saskatchewan 1905

1905-1910 Amédée E. Forget
1910-1915 George W. Brown
1915-1921 Sir Richard Lake
1921-1931 Henry W. Newlands
1931-1936 Hugh E. Munroe
1936-1945 Archibald Peter McNab
1945 Thomas Miller

1945-1948	Reginald J.M. Parker
1948-1951	John Michael Uhrich
1951-1958	William J. Patterson
1958-1963	Frank Lindsay Bastedo
1963-1970	Robert L. Hanbidge
1970-1976	Stephen Worobetz
1976-1977	George Porteous
1978-	C. Irwin McIntosh

Alberta 1905

1905-1915	George H.V. Bulyea
1915-1925	Robert George Brett
1925-1931	William Egbert
1931-1936	William L. Walsh
1936-1937	Philip C.H. Primrose
1937-1950	John Campbell Bowen
1950-1959	John James Bowlen
1959-1969	John Percy Page
1969-1974	J.W. Grant MacEwan
1974-	Ralph Steinhauer

Newfoundland 1949

1729-1731	Henry Osborne
1731	George Clinton
1732	Edward Falkingham
1733-1734	Lord Muskerry
1735-1737	Fitzroy Lee
1738	Philip Vanbrugh
1739	Henry Medley
1740	Lord George Graham
1741, 1743	Thomas Smith
1742	John Byng
1744	Charles Hardy
1745	Richard Edwards
1748	Charles Watson
1749	George B. Rodney
1750-1752	Francis W. Drake
1753-1754	Hugh Bonfoy
1755-1756	Richard Dorrill
1757-1759	Richard Edwards
1760-1761	James Webb
1761-1763	Thomas Graves
1764-1768	Hugh Palliser
1769-1772	John Byron
1772-1774	Molyneux Shuldham
1775-1776	Robert Duff
1776-1778	John Montagu
1779-1781	Richard Edwards
1782-1786	John Campbell
1786-1789	John Elliott
1789-1792	Mark Milbanke
1792-1794	Sir Richard King
1794-1797	Sir James Wallace
1797-1800	William Waldegrave
1800-1801	Sir Charles M. Pole
1802-1804	James Gambier
1804-1806	Sir Erasmus Gower
1807-1809	John Holloway
1810-1813	Sir John T. Duckworth
1813-1816	Sir Richard Godwin Keats
1816-1818	Sir Francis Pickmore
1818-1824	Sir Charles Hamilton
1825-1834	Sir Thomas John Cochrane
1834-1841	Henry Prescott
1841-1846	Sir John Harvey
1847-1852	Sir John Sheppard LeMarchant
1852-1855	Ker Baillie Hamilton
1855-1857	Charles Henry Darling
1857-1863	Sir Alexander Bannerman
1864-1869	Sir Anthony Musgrave
1869-1875	Sir Stephen Hill
1875-1881, 1883-1886	Sir John H. Glover
1881-1883	Sir Henry F.B. Maxse
1886-1887	Sir George William Desvoeux
1887-1888	Sir Henry A. Blake
1888-1895	Sir John T.H. O'Brien
1895-1898	Sir Herbert Hailey Murray
1898-1901	Sir Henry E. McCallum
1901-1904	Sir Cavendish Boyle
1904-1909	Sir William MacGregor
1909-1913	Sir Ralph C. Williams
1913-1917	Sir Walter E. Davidson
1917-1922	Sir Charles A. Harris
1922-1928	Sir William Allardyce
1928-1932	Sir John Middleton
1932-1936	Sir David M. Anderson
1936-1946	Humphry L. Walwyn
1946-1949	Sir Gordon MacDonald
1949	Sir Albert J. Walsh
1949-1957	Sir Leonard Outerbridge
1957-1963	Campbell L. Macpherson
1963-1971	Fabian O'Dea
1971-1974	E. John H. Harnum
1974-	Gordon A. Winter

Notes

1 A pageantry rooted in our history

PAGE 9, LINE 12
Dufferin-Carnarvon Correspondence, C.W. de Kiewiet and F.H. Underhill, eds. (Toronto, Champlain Society, 1955), p. 174.

2 Head of state and head of government

PAGE 17, LINE 6
Le Devoir, Montréal, 12 octobre 1964. "Le rôle de la monarchie constitutionelle est de personnifier l'état démocratique." Author's translation.

PAGE 19, LINE 1
Vincent Massey, *On Being Canadian* (Toronto, Dent, 1948), p. 60.

PAGE 19, LINE 14
Parliamentary Debates on the Subject of the Confederation of the British North American Provinces. (Quebec, 1865), p. 62.

PAGE 20, LINE 6
Ibid., p. 33.

PAGE 20, LINE 30
La Presse, Montréal, 25 février, 1966. "En sa personne, l'autorité civile se montrait à la fois élevée et familière, soucieuse de semer la joie autant que d'inspirer le respect. Il importe qu'au-dessus des discussions nécessaires et des heurts inévitables dans une société démocratique, l'autorité civile, don divin, apparaisse dans toute sa richesse et qu'elle soit non seulement forte et noble, mais acueillante et aimable." Author's translation.

PAGE 23, LINE 5
Edits, Ordonnances royaux (Québec, 1854) I, p. 7. "Tant et si avant qu'ils pourront étendre et faire connaître le nom de Sa Majesté." Author's translation.

PAGE 23, LINE 19
W.J. Eccles, *Canada Under Louis XIV* (Toronto, McClelland and Stewart, 1964), p. xi.

PAGE 26, LINE 24
In 1906 this was converted to $48,666.63, which is still the salary paid to the Governor General.

3 A Canadian choice

PAGE 32, LINE 11
Senate Debates, March 29, 1972, p. 278.

PAGE 34, LINE 24
Parliamentary Debates, op. cit., p. 34.

PAGE 37, LINE 9
Imperial Conference 1926, Summary of Proceedings (Canada, Sessional Paper 10, 1926-27), Pt. VI, "Inter-Imperial Relations."

PAGE 43, LINE 7
Lord Fitzgerald in *Hodge* v. *The Queen* (1883) App. Cas. 117.

PAGE 44, LINE 16
Lord Watson in *Liquidators of the Maritime Bank of Canada* v. *The Receiver General of New Brunswick* (1892) App. Cas. 437, pp. 441 ff. Quoted in J.M. Beck, *The Shaping of Canadian Federalism: Central Authority or Provincial Right?* (Toronto, Copp Clark, 1971), pp. 94-6.

PAGE 45, LINE 17
As quoted in *The Guardian*, Charlottetown, July 19, 1975.

4 Royal responsibilities

PAGE 51, LINE 20
R.L. Cheffins and R.N. Tucker, *The Constitutional Process in Canada*, 2nd edition (Toronto, McGraw-Hill Ryerson, 1975), p. 78.

PAGE 52, LINE 18
Frank MacKinnon, *The Crown in Canada* (Calgary, McClelland and Stewart West, 1976), p. 122.

PAGE 54, LINE 5
The Hon. Eugene Forsey, "No Figurehead, Governor General's duties and powers clear," *The Citizen*, Ottawa, January 23, 1974, p. 6.

PAGE 56, LINE 4
Cheffins and Tucker, *op. cit.*, p. 88, and MacKinnon, *op. cit.*, p. 127.

PAGE 56, LINE 12
The Globe and Mail, Toronto, December 2, 1971.

PAGE 57, LINE 25
MacKinnon, *op. cit.*, p. 127.

PAGE 58, LINE 14
Eugene A. Forsey, *The Royal Power of Dissolution of Parliament in the British Commonwealth* (Toronto, Oxford University Press, 1968), pp. 270-71.

PAGE 59, LINE 19
Eugene Forsey, "The Crown and the Constitution," *Dalhousie Review*, Spring, 1953, p. 137.

PAGE 64, LINE 1
J.M. Hendry, *Memorandum on the Office of Lieutenant Governor of a Province. Its Constitutional character and functions* (Ottawa, Ministry of Justice, 1955), p. 23.

PAGE 64, LINE 11
See *ibid.*, p. 24.

PAGE 66, LINE 6
Quoted in Harold Nicholson, *George V, His Life and Reign* (London, Pan Books Ltd., 1952), pp. 99-100.

PAGE 67, LINE 4
From notes for the speech given by the Prime Minister of Canada at the Installation of the Right Honourable Jules Léger in the Senate, January 14, 1974.

PAGE 68, LINE 23
The Hon. Pauline McGibbon, "The Role of the Lieutenant Governor," an Address in the Sir Sandford Fleming College Lecture Series for Women, Peterborough, November 19, 1975.

PAGE 69, LINE 3
From the CBC-TV documentary "The Canadian Monarchy," broadcast November 23, 1977.

PAGE 69, LINE 7
Quoted in *The Journal*, Ottawa, January 9, 1974.

PAGE 69, LINE 12
Robert Borden, "The Imperial Conference," *Journal of the Royal Institute of International Affairs*, July, 1927, p. 204.

PAGE 70, LINE 1
Peter C. Newman, "Massey's Thoughts on Canada," *Montreal Star*, February 25, 1967.

PAGE 71, LINE 26
The Rt. Hon. Roland Michener, "Looking back at Rideau Hall," *Historical Papers*, 1975, p. 140.

PAGE 73, LINE 18
J.R. Mallory, "The appointment of the Governor General: Responsible Government, autonomy, and the Royal Prerogative," *The Canadian Journal of Economics and Political Science*, February, 1960, p. 106.

5 *A symbol of our community*

PAGE 77, LINE 6
The Governor General's standard was approved by King George V in 1931 and may have been suggested by him personally as early as 1928. The Queen's standard was approved for her personal use in Canada in August, 1962. The Lieutenant Governors, except those of Quebec and Saskatchewan, all use a design based on the Union Jack and originally authorized by Queen Victoria in 1869. Quebec uses a flag approved in the mid 1950s and Saskatchewan has no official flag for the Lieutenant Governor.

PAGE 80, LINE 26
As quoted by Y. Zoltvany, "Philippe Rigaud de Vaudreuil" in *Dictionary of Canadian Biography*, Vol II (Toronto, University of Toronto Press, 1969), p.573.

PAGE 81, LINE 3
The Leader-Post, Regina, January 28, 1970.

PAGE 81, LINE 8
As quoted by Hilda Neatby in *Quebec, The Revolutionary Age, 1760-1791* (Toronto, McClelland and Stewart, 1966), p. 26.

Photo Credits

Every effort has been made to acknowledge correctly the sources of the illustrations reproduced in this book. The publishers welcome any information which will enable them to rectify, in subsequent editions, any errors or omissions which may have been made in crediting the pictures.

PAC: Public Archives Canada

Page 9, PAC C 1014; 10 and 11, Capital Press Service, Ottawa; 12, NFB Photothèque ONF ©; 13 (left), PAC; 13 (right), Confederation Life Collection; 14, NFB Photothèque ONF ©; 15 (left) PAC C 2294; 15 (right, upper and lower), PAC C 50506; 16 (upper), PAC PA 9638; 17, PAC C 21398; 18, Confederation Life Collection; 19, PAC C 21873; 20, PAC C 30277; 21 (left), PAC PA 32846; 21 (right), PAC PA 47027; 22 and 23 (left), Confederation Life Collection; 23 (right), PAC C 98874; 24 (left), PAC Simpson I-7; 24 (right), PAC PA 29981; 25 PAC C 14305; 26, PAC C 33195; 27 (left), PAC C 539; 27 (centre), PAC C 561; 27 (right), PAC 9014; 28 (upper), PAC C 11043; 28 (lower), PAC C 6737; 29 (left), PAC C 28393; 29 (right), PAC C 13070; 30 (right), NFB Photothèque ONF ©; 31, Archives of Ontario L1654; 32, PAC C 4665; 33 (left), PAC 1023; 33 (right), PAC C 23912; 34, PAC PA 29060; 35, PAC C 11508; 36, PAC C 9061; 37, PAC C 61621; 38 (left), Capital Press Service, Ottawa; 38 (right), Karsh, Ottawa; 39 (left), John Evans; 40 (left), Archives of Ontario S293; 40 (right), PAC C 18810; 41 (lower left), PAC C 3216; 41 (upper left), Karsh, Ottawa; 45 (left), Cavouk, The Colonnade; 45 (right), UPI Photo; 46 and 47, Capital Press Service, Ottawa; 48 (left), NFB Photothèque ONF ©; 48 (right), Province of New Brunswick Photo; 49 (lower), PAC C 6792; 49 (upper), PAC C 33866; 50 (upper left), PAC C 26996; 50 (lower left), PAC C 23330; 50 (right), NFB Photothèque ONF ©; 51, CP Photo; 52, PAC C 25691; 54, Lady Stanley's albums; 56, PAC PA 26577; 57, PAC C 27345; 58, PAC PA 30903; 60, PAC PA 41391; 61 and 62 (both), John Evans; 63 (right), PAC C 98879; 63 (centre), PAC C 98880; 63 (left), Dominion Wide; 64 (left), Michael Burns, Toronto; 64 (right), Photo Features; 65 (right), PAC C 19930; 66, *Le Droit*; 67, PAC PA 25088; 68 (right), Lady Bessborough's albums; 69 (left), Fednews; 69 (right), *The Gazette*, Montreal; 70 (upper left), PAC PA 100363; 70 (right), NFB Photothèque ONF ©; 73, *Le Droit*; 75 (left), Queen's University Archives; 75 (lower right), PAC; 75 (upper right), Dave Paterson; 76 (upper left), PAC PA 20798; 77 (lower right), Gilbert Milne Photography; 77 (upper right), PAC PA 98903; 78 (centre), Arnott Rogers Batten Ltd.; 78 (lower left), PAC C 6378; 78 (upper left), PAC C 11569; 79 (left), Photo Features; 80 (left), private collection; 80 (centre), PAC C 26920; 80 (right), Capital Press Service, Ottawa; 81 (top right), PAC C 10614; 81 (lower right), PAC; 82, CP Photo; Cover (both), NFB Photothèque ONF ©.

The author would like to thank the secretaries to the Lieutenant Governors for their gracious assistance in obtaining photographs, and in supplying the list of the Lieutenant Governors of Newfoundland, prepared at Memorial University.

Index